THE Secrets AND Simple Truths OF High-Performing School Cultures

THE Secrets AND Simple Truths OF High-Performing School Cultures

CATHY J. LASSITER

LEAD+
LEARN
PRESS

ENGLEWOOD, COLORADO

The Leadership and Learning Center
317 Inverness Way South, Suite 150
Englewood, Colorado 80112
Phone 1.866.399.6019 | Fax 303.504.9417
www.LeadandLearn.com

Published by Lead + Learn Press, a division of Houghton Mifflin Harcourt.

Library of Congress Cataloging-in-Publication Data

Lassiter, Cathy J.
The secrets and simple truths of high-performing school cultures / Cathy J. Lassiter.
p. cm.
Includes bibliographical references and index.
ISBN 978-1-935588-32-0 (alk. paper)
1. School improvement programs. 2. School environment. 3. Educational leadership. 4. Learning, Psychology of. I. Title.
LB2822.8.L37 2012
371.2'07—dc23

2012004561

ISBN 978-1-935588-32-0
Printed in the United States of America

16 15 14 13 12 01 02 03 04 05 06 07

DEDICATION

To the most wonderful young people in the world,
Brittany and Blake, who are indeed their mother's joy.

To Tim, the most understanding, kind, and patient husband.

To the best parents a child could ever have, Billy and Scarlett.

Contents

Acknowledgments

Many people have supported, guided, and assisted in the production of this book. Kristin Anderson's positive patience and genuine interest in my success have served as an anchor to steady my work and help me maintain appropriate focus. Brian McNulty and Ainsley Rose have shared their expertise and insight. Their kind words, encouragement, and knowledge were invaluable to the content and organization of the book. Katie Stoddard was always available to give guidance and feedback for improvement. Linda O'Konek has been a friend through thick and thin, good and bad, both in the district where we worked for many years and as a colleague at The Center. Former superintendent John Simpson and Superintendent Melinda Boone for their leadership, guidance, and outstanding modeling of courage and strength. Lil Thomas for her support, praise, and continued friendship.

Finally, enormous gratitude goes to Douglas Reeves, founder of The Leadership and Learning Center. He has achieved a level of success and credibility in the field that most of us can only dream about. At the same time, he finds time to offer his expertise and best advice to many. Because of the support from Dr. Reeves, I am able to work in an organization that provides me with the greatest professional satisfaction of my 29-year career in education. I can never repay him for that. I can only offer my humble appreciation.

Preface

Does intrinsic motivation exist and, if so, how powerful can it be in influencing the work of principals and teachers? This is the question that kept swirling in my head after reading *Drive: The Surprising Truth About What Motivates Us* by Daniel Pink and led me on the journey that has resulted in this book. I was fascinated with the "puzzling puzzles" of Harry Harlow, described by Pink in the book's first chapter. Harry Harlow was a pioneer in behavioral science research in the early 1950s, focusing primarily on human emotions and infants' attachment to their mothers. During my reading about his experiment on puzzling puzzles, I recalled learning about a Harlow experiment while in college that involved monkeys in cages: one had a wire mother figure and one had a cloth mother figure.

Harlow published his observations of how the infant monkeys reacted to both. But the experiment mentioned by Pink that involved the monkeys and a three-step mechanical device was one with which I was not familiar. This research involved observing the monkeys when the device was placed in their cages. Harlow found the monkeys' reactions to be quite surprising and literally groundbreaking in the field of psychology. The monkeys responded to the mechanical device by immediately touching it, looking at it, moving its parts, and working intently to figure out how it worked. They worked persistently until they were able to perform the device's three steps and unhook it. According to Harlow, the monkeys seemed to derive great satisfaction and enjoyment from performing the three steps to open the latch. They did it over and over again and got faster and faster at the task. They were not taught how to unlatch the device; did not receive any reward, either food or drink, for their performance; and they were not demonstrating behaviors researchers had seen before. Why were the monkeys so driven to solve the puzzle? What internal drive caused their persistence and determination to conquer the challenge? What enjoyment could they derive from the task?

Harlow then decided to experiment with giving rewards to the monkeys as they solved the puzzle. He wanted to know if offering rewards would improve the monkeys' performance. Would they get faster and better at the three steps? He decided to provide raisins as a reward for performance. Much to his surprise, the reward of raisins actually seemed to diminish the monkeys' motivation for the task. They made more errors and became less interested in performing the task. They became more interested in the raisins and less interested in the three-step process for opening the latch on the device. Harlow concluded that solving the puzzle or conquering the challenge provided what he termed "intrinsic motivation" for the monkeys. He suggested that this intrinsic motivation also existed in human beings and that rewards and punishments might not be the best way to motivate a human workforce. His radical idea was met with much skepticism and resistance from colleagues in the field as, prior to Harlow, there were only two human drives known to exist: one for food and water and the other for sexual or carnal urges. This newly identified drive for solving a puzzle or conquering a challenge, as suggested by Harlow, was not accepted in research circles until much later. We now know that Harlow was indeed on to something about what drives human behavior; in fact, his observations and conclusions were spot-on.

After learning about Harlow's experiment, I decided to do my own crude test of his findings on intrinsic motivation and use my sixteen-year-old son as the guinea pig. I set up my experiment using one of those wooden brainteaser puzzles so popular today. The puzzle consisted of six wooden pieces that, when assembled correctly, formed a multipointed star (see Figure P.1).

I left the wooden pieces on the kitchen counter and waited for my unsuspecting son to come home from school. Right on schedule, he arrived home and tossed his book bag onto the floor. He noticed the wooden pieces on the counter and asked about them. Perfect, I thought, my experiment on intrinsic motivation is about to begin. I told him that the pieces were a brainteaser puzzle that I planned to use in a workshop. He asked me if he could try to put it together. Of course, with my observation skills ready to kick in, I told him he could. He took the puzzle over to a chair and began work. He focused intently on the task. He worked it from many different angles. He seemed to enjoy it. I asked him several times if I could assist him. He promptly rejected any help

FIGURE P.1 **Six-Piece Brainteaser Puzzle**

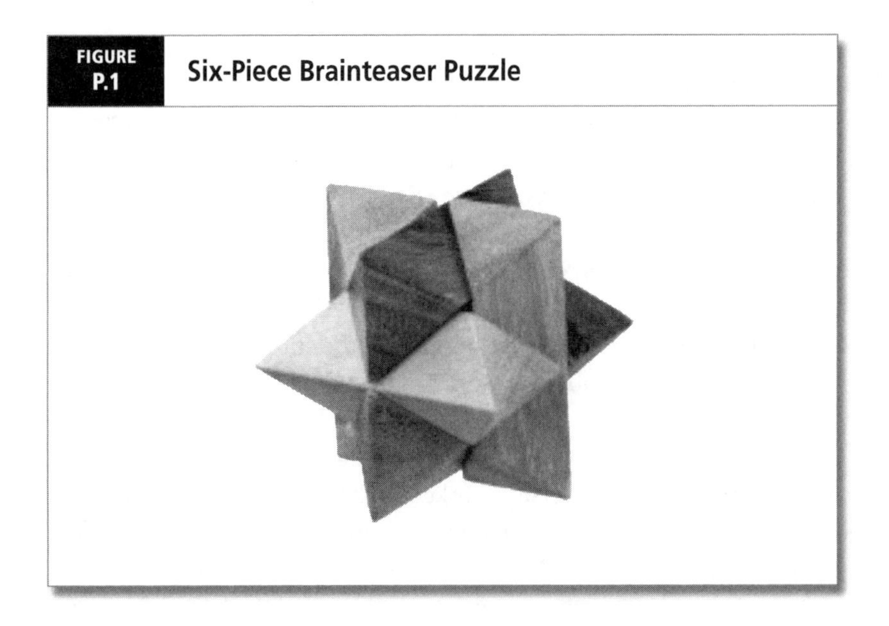

from me. I informed him that he could go to YouTube and see a video on how to solve it. He promptly rejected that notion as well. He said he wanted to solve it himself. I had offered him no reward for his hard work. He would receive no money, no gold star, no blue ribbon, no certificate, no trophy, no pat on the back; and yet, he worked intently and seriously at solving the puzzle. It was remarkable to me, as he had *never* worked like this on any homework assignment! After some time had passed, he finally solved it. He enthusiastically did the Tiger Woods fist pump and said, "Yes! I did it!" It is important to note that this child, while being a good student, does not live and die based on his schoolwork performance or grade point average (GPA). Why did he focus so intently on this task, just like the monkeys in Harlow's experiment? Was he intrinsically motivated to conquer a challenge? I had to expand my experimentation to find out.

My next experiment again involved my unsuspecting son and several of his friends as well. The boys were coming to our house to play their favorite Xbox game. I placed a number of the wooden puzzles on the table where they would be playing and waited to see what would happen. The boys asked my son about the wooden pieces. When he told them they were pieces from a brainteaser puzzle, each of them immediately picked up six pieces and began work on solving the puzzle. They did not play Xbox, did not have snacks, and did not have drinks. They worked as intently as my son had on his first try with the puzzle. Again, following each boy's success with the puzzle, the fist pumps, high fives, and in-zone dances ensued. The whole scene was fascinating to watch. Here were typical sixteen-year-old high school students focused and working on putting six wooden pieces together to form a star. Why? Again, I had "proved" ever so unscientifically that Harlow and all the subsequent behaviorists were correct in their notion that human beings have three drives, one of which is to conquer a challenge or solve a puzzle.

My experimentation continued and included my daughter, a freshman at Virginia Tech University; workers at the UPS store where I do business; colleagues at The Leadership and Learning Center; and hundreds of school leaders who attended conferences where I was their presenter. Each and every time these varied groups of people picked up the puzzle pieces, they worked intently and persistently until they had conquered the challenge. At no time was there a reward offered for their success. They were motivated internally to complete the task, solve the puzzle, conquer the challenge, and derived great joy and satisfaction in doing so.

The research by Harlow on drive, plus additional research by Pink on purpose, vision, and mission, together with my own reading, research, and experience in education, have led me to this place at this time. I have since gone deeper with my research on the subject and made several discoveries along the way that intrigued me and reinforced my own knowledge about what it takes to create and sustain a culture of high performance in schools. I have framed this book around both past and surprising new research on human behavior and motivation, as well as on my 29 years of experience as a school principal, central office administrator, and educational consultant in districts around the country. I encourage readers to conduct their own informal experimentation on intrinsic motivation, drive, purpose, and challenge and learn from their results. This most certainly is not scholarly research, but it is fascinating to observe and interesting to consider the implications of this work for school leaders. It is through this lens that I offer the following chapters on high-performance school cultures.

Introduction

If you examine the leadership section in your local bookstore or take a tour through Amazon.com, you know immediately that there are many books written about leadership and culture. Each takes a different twist or angle to set it apart from the rest in an effort to help interested leaders perform better in their roles. This book attempts to look at the issues through a different perspective—one you have not read before, one that will both surprise you and reinforce some often-neglected tried and proven truths. By combining recent research in science—specifically in psychology, biology, and economics—with business and educational research, we discover some secrets not widely known or understood and some simple truths of what makes a school culture high performing.

The culture of an organization is founded upon the assumptions, beliefs, values, and habits that constitute the norms for that organization. Norms shape how people think, feel, and act (DuFour and Eaker, 1998, p. 131). The concept of changing the culture of a school may seem simple enough on the surface, but when you begin talking about and pushing people to examine highly personal beliefs, expectations, biases, and habits that have gone unaddressed, the complexity of changing a culture becomes painfully clear. Yet, for those who understand that their cultures must change for the good of students, or that the culture must change in order to keep the school from being closed, or that the culture must change in order to meet ever-increasing accountability demands, the path is clear. It will be messy, challenging, instructional, and rewarding.

With this book, I endeavor to inspire new thinking on the topic and to encourage new actions on the part of school leaders at every level to think deeply about the importance of their culture as they move forward to tackle the challenging demands coming their way. Ken Blanchard describes high-performing organizations as enterprises that, over time, continue to produce outstanding results with the highest level of human satisfaction and commitment to success (Blanchard, 2007, p. 10).

Blanchard includes a compelling vision as one of the hallmarks of a high-performance organization. He says:

> When everyone supports an organization's vision—including purpose, picture of the future, and values—it creates a deliberate highly focused culture that drives the desired results toward a greater good. In these organizations, people are energized by and excited about and dedicated to such a vision. They have a noble sense of purpose that creates and focuses energy. (Blanchard, 2007, p. 11)

But what Blanchard does not include in his description is the science behind why this is true. Part One of the book examines the secrets of human behavior, known to scientists in the fields of psychology, evolutionary biology, political science, sociology, mathematical biology, and others, but not readily known by most educators. This unexpected and interesting new information is presented as "secrets" to creating a high-performing school culture. The three secrets of high-performance cultures, gleaned from brand-new and recent research from the sciences, are as follows:

- Humans are driven internally to seek purpose and conquer challenges.
- A few vital behaviors can change the world.
- Cooperation and collaboration are evolutionary.

Each of the secrets is described through the lens of scientific research and examined for its impact on school culture. Examples are provided from schools and districts that have discovered and applied these secrets and have successfully created high-performance cultures in their organizations.

Part Two focuses on a few of the most powerful simple truths or known facts that are staples in educational research but are often overlooked or taken for granted. In many cases, these simple truths have gone dormant in the field, and school leaders have forgotten their plain and simple influence on the culture of a school. Leaders need to understand that three simple truths should form the bedrock of their school cultures, and these truths need to be tended vigilantly in order for them to flourish. These simple truths get to the heart of what people believe about data, accountability, teaching, and leadership. As well, these truths have a significant impact on a school's culture and provide significant leverage in creating a high-performance culture. The three simple truths are:

- Teaching talent makes the difference.
- Leaders cannot do it alone.
- Data and accountability are critical friends.

These simple truths may seem obvious, but that is precisely the point. Everyone in education can agree with the truths as facts; but what do they *do* with the information? How do they act on these truths in a way that makes a difference in the culture of the school? Would their staff members agree that these truths are understood and implemented deeply at the school?

These secrets and simple truths should provoke leaders to reflect on the culture in their schools and encourage a sense of urgency to apply them in meaningful ways to develop a high-performance culture for the good of the staff, students, and communities they serve.

Part Three of the book makes the case for why culture is so important at this point in time. With the continuing crisis in the economy, the demands for schools to compete more successfully on international assessments, the changes to No Child Left Behind (NCLB), and the adoption and implementation of the Common Core State Standards (CCSS) and accompanying national assessments, schools must focus on culture to face a new generation of challenges effectively. If the culture is not built upon and does not fully utilize these three secrets and simple truths, it will not be flexible enough to keep up with change.

Finally, the book concludes with applying the lessons from the secrets and simple truths to create a high-performing culture. Specifically, a culture that embraces challenge, works together for the greater good, grows and learns together, uses data to make decisions, and shares accountability for results. Building this kind of culture is the only path to success for schools, as the expectations and demands for results ramp up with the Common Core State Standards and next-generation assessments. Readers will find suggested strategies and activities for each of the secrets and simple truths they can use at faculty meetings, leadership meetings, and other gatherings of staff that will help them apply what they have learned in this book. Successful application and implementation of the secrets and simple truths will result in a culture that exemplifies the characteristics of the high-performance school cultures described throughout the book.

PART ONE

The *Secrets* to Creating a High-Performance School Culture

CHAPTER ONE

HPC SECRET 1: Humans Are Driven to Seek Purpose and Conquer Challenges

In a world of information overload and centrifugal goals, employees and organizations often spin away from their basic sense of purpose and direction. Great leaders recognize what motivates employees, match employee motivators to organizational purposes, and help employees prioritize work that matters most.

Dave and Wendy Ulrich, *The Why of Work: How Great Leaders Build Abundant Organizations That Win*

REWARDS AND PUNISHMENTS

Reward-and-punishment, or carrot-and-stick accountability programs, are not the answer to school underperformance, and the research is very clear on this fact. Let's begin with the work of Teresa Amabile, a professor and researcher at Harvard's Business School. Her work on motivation and job satisfaction suggests that external rewards and punishments—that is, carrots and sticks—can be effective in motivating workers who perform highly routine tasks, because the work is boring and monotonous, and few people aspire to spend their lives engaged in this type of work. But in knowledge-based work, where people are faced with solving complex challenges, creating novel approaches to age-old problems, and developing new, creative strategies to get ahead, carrots and sticks have no positive influence on worker motivation or productivity.

In fact, in jobs where people must think and act creatively, extrinsic motivation is detrimental (Amabile, 1996). In one study, Amabile and several colleagues tested the if–then motivational theory using commissioned and noncommissioned pieces of artwork from various artists in the United States. The researchers asked a panel of art experts to judge the pieces for creativity and skill. The results were very telling. The noncommissioned pieces were deemed to be substantially more creative than and equal in skill to the commissioned pieces. The researchers concluded that work created from self-motivation, absent of rewards and punishments, void of if–then scenarios, is more productive, creative, and satisfying to the worker.

This is not to say that people work entirely for intrinsic motives. They do indeed need to be able to earn a living, send their children to college, and enjoy their time off. However, as Daniel Pink describes in *Drive: The Surprising Truth About What Motivates Us*, once a person has achieved a comfortable baseline salary, carrots and sticks can have the counterintended effect of squelching the individual's intrinsic motivation toward his work (Pink, 2009). Once the baseline salary is achieved, people move beyond salary as a reward and on to higher concerns and aspirations. They are programmed at birth to seek purpose and challenge in their work; it is part of human nature. "This is one of the most robust findings in the social sciences—and also one of the most ignored" (Pink, 2009, p. 39). "For artists, scientists, inventors, schoolchildren, and the rest of us, intrinsic motivation—the drive to do something because it is interesting, challenging, and absorbing—is essential for high levels of creativity" (Pink, 2009, p. 43). According to Michael Fullan's newest work, *Change Leader: Learning to Do What Matters Most*, "you can't make people change, and rewards and punishment either don't work or are short lived—the only thing that works is people's intrinsic motivation, and you have to get at this indirectly" (Fullan, 2011, p. 51). Affirming this, Daniel Pink writes, "the 'if–then' motivators that are the staple of most organizations often stifle, rather than stir, creative thinking" (Pink, 2009, p. 46).

THE DRIVE TO ACHIEVE

If we consider the findings in Harlow's experiments, mentioned in the preface, as well as the subsequent and substantive research since then, we have to consider the following: all human beings are driven to succeed at work that makes a difference, each person strives for meaning and purpose at work, and each worker desires to do good work. Work is not simply a mechanism by which to earn a salary. Rather, work is a vehicle for personal or internal satisfaction and fulfillment.

In fact, in research conducted by Jim Collins, author of *Good to Great*, and his colleague Morten Hansen, superior performance in pursuit of being a great organization is indeed a "human quest"(2011, p. 12). The purpose of their research, chronicled in *Great by Choice: Uncertainty, Chaos, and Luck—Why Some Thrive Despite Them All*, was to identify the highest-performing organizations that sustained significant growth during times of change, challenge, and crisis. Of the 20,000-plus companies they reviewed, seven were celebrated as 10X organizations—that is, organizations that posted growth at 10 times the rate of organizations in their comparison group. Data on the decisions, practices, and personal attributes of the leaders were analyzed and reported in the book.

The findings support the works previously cited. Collins and Hansen write,

> Every 10Xer we studied aimed for much more than just "becoming successful." They didn't define themselves by money. They didn't define themselves by fame. They didn't define themselves by power. They defined themselves by impact and contribution and purpose. (p. 33)

The authors go on suggest that the greatest leaders, those that post exceptional organizational performance for sustained periods of time, in this case for 15 years or more, are very much focused on the greater good. They want to motivate and inspire people to do work that makes a difference in the world. A difference that will be sustained and endure even after they are all gone from the organization. These 10Xer leaders created cultures that were characterized as "cult like," where the right people were empowered to flourish and learn, and the wrong people self- ejected. Additionally, the writers emphasize that 10Xer leaders are fanatical about getting the right people on their teams, and that having the right people was the number one strategy for meeting their goals and achieving great outcomes. We will discuss the importance of finding and keeping the right people in more detail in Chapter Four.

According to Dave and Wendy Ulrich, authors of *The Why of Work: How Great Leaders Build Abundant Organizations That Win*, leaders of all organizations can indeed bring the kind of purpose and direction discussed in Collins and Hansen to their organizations. They must create structures and opportunities for employees to think about and share their ideas on four critical categories that speak to purpose. These are: insight, achievement, connection, and empowerment (Ulrich and Ulrich, 2010). A leader can pose the following questions to people in their organization to establish the collective purpose and appropriate challenges for the work. Consider these questions:

- What are the insights we need to succeed as an organization?
- What achievements and goals will keep us in business?
- What types of relationships will help us get our work done?
- What human problems are we trying to solve?
- What are the most pressing motivations of this organization?

(Ulrich and Ulrich, 2010, pp. 101–102)

When we engage in thinking about why we do the work we do and what we hope to achieve by doing it, we engage in purpose thinking. The more frequent the conversation about purpose, the more likely people will feel a connection to it and become engaged fully in the work. Commitment and drive to achieve go up and job satisfaction will also be high. Leaders must establish a clear line of sight between the work of every individual in the organization and the purpose of the organization. This purpose motive will bring people together naturally as they strive toward an outcome none could achieve individually.

DOING "GOOD WORK"

School leaders and leaders of other nonprofit organizations should be able to establish this connection quite easily, as there is a built-in moral purpose in the work of teachers, nurses, firefighters, and the like. Nonprofit institutions exist for the sake of their mission. They exist to make a difference in society and in the life of the individual. The first task of the nonprofit leader is to make sure everybody sees the mission, hears it, and lives it (Drucker, 1990). But the reality today is that leaders develop and distribute a mission statement and *assume* employees will go forth and make it happen. The daily work of all staff is not explicitly linked to the mission, people do not know their individual roles in achieving the mission, and they see no real connection in their work to a higher purpose or greater good. This is a huge missed opportunity for leaders, especially school leaders. Peter Drucker argues the mission has to be clear and simple. It has to be bigger than any one person's capacity. It has to lift up people's vision. It has to be something that makes each person feel that he or she can make a difference—that each one can say, "I have not lived in vain" (Drucker, 1990).

Although education is infused with an important moral and policy purpose, it remains critical to make explicit links between the daily work of teachers, the purpose of the school, and the greater good to the community (Curtis and Wurtzel, 2010). This notion of the "greater good" is heavily referenced in the literature on motivation. In two separate studies conducted 25 years apart in the United Kingdom and Sweden, separate researchers tested the greater good theory by examining donors' motivations for giving blood. They concluded that people are more strongly motivated to donate blood if they feel as though it is for the good of the citizenry. Making a contribution to something bigger than themselves, something for the greater good, serves as a strong motivational force. Donating blood voluntarily provides donors with what the American Red Cross describes as a feeling money cannot buy (Pink, 2009).

School leaders are in a prime position to inspire this feeling that money cannot buy in their faculties by keeping the purpose and mission alive in their actions, recognizing team members for work aligned with the mission, including examples of "good work" in all communications, and by making all decisions through the lens of the purpose or mission. Doing good work feels good. As long as the job provides clear goals, immediate feedback, and a level of challenge matching our skills, we have a chance to experience work as "good" (Gardner, Csikszentmihalyi, and Damon, 2002). Fullan argues, ". . . it is in situations where we actually accomplish something of high moral value, which in turn energizes us to do even more. It is being in the moment of a successful endeavor that fuels passion, not just dreaming of it" (Fullan, 2011, p. 23). Failure to make this connection leads to consequences such as the exodus of veteran and new teachers for jobs that provide a stronger sense of purpose, challenge, and recognition of good work (Curtis and Wurtzel, 2010).

Additional research that supports this axiom was conducted by Mid-continent Research for Education and Learning in 2001 (McREL). This four-year study examined how high-poverty, high-performing schools beat the odds. They identified 739 high-performing schools and 738 low-performing schools, all of whom had 50 percent or more of their students on free or reduced-price lunch. Their findings support the importance of vision and purpose to school improvement efforts. The Beat-the-Odds schools developed, with input from teachers, a vision of success and a clear focus for their improvement efforts. The researchers also found that both the high- and low-performing schools focused on many of the same strategies for improvement, such as assessment, monitoring, collaboration, and professional development (Goodwin, 2010).

The culture in which this work takes place is what separates the high- from the low-performing schools. The high performers' vision and mission enabled them to create a web or network of connected reform strategies that helped establish a purpose motive. It provided a clear answer to why we do the work we do. It established a clear goal and destination, as opposed to an isolated set of actions for teacher compliance, as was the case in the low-performing schools. An organization's vision and mission should compel employee commitment and engagement. Engaged employees want their organization to succeed because they feel connected emotionally and socially to the mission, vision, and purpose.

VISION 2020 AT COCA-COLA

About a year ago, the Coca-Cola Company created their long-term vision project entitled Vision 2020. The resulting work provides an interesting example of how a highly profitable global brand has capitalized on the research on what motivates human beings: to engage in good work with a clear purpose motive. The company Web site includes this statement about their mission: "Our roadmap starts with our mission, which is enduring. It declares our purpose as a company and serves as the standard against which we weigh our actions and decisions." They go on to describe the Coca-Cola mission, which contains three clear, powerful statements that are purpose driven. They are: 1. Refresh the world; 2. Inspire moments of optimism and happiness; and 3. Create value and make a difference.

These statements have little to do with beverage distribution. However, they provide a challenge and purpose to the company's workers worldwide that engages them in working toward the greater good (www.coca-cola.com). Remember, this is a soft-drink company, not a nonprofit community service organization. Clearly, company leaders are leveraging the human desire for good work and the yearning for purpose and challenge in their jobs. School leaders, by the nature of the work, have a more direct connection to the greater good and, therefore, should be able to create a purpose-driven mission and vision that exceed that of a soft-drink company.

VISION AT WHITTIER UNION HIGH SCHOOL DISTRICT, CALIFORNIA

One such leader is Sandra Thorstenson, Superintendent of Whittier Union High School District in California. The mission for this high-performing district is to "achieve and maintain excellence in providing a comprehensive education for all students" (www.wuhsd.org). In short, this district strives to provide an excellent education for each student they serve. In addition to the mission, the district has a set of belief statements that describe how their mind-set about themselves, their colleagues, the students, and their parents will impact their achievement of the mission. They believe every student can learn, every student has worth and dignity, and every student must be prepared to meet the challenges and changing needs of society. In her letter to the community to kick off the 2010–2011 school year, Superintendent Thorstenson writes: "I want you to know that all of us at Whittier Union remain steadfastly dedicated to doing everything we can to ensure our students' well-being and academic achievement and that they not only attain, but also surpass our expectations of what they can achieve" (www. wuhsd.org).

Through these beliefs and this mind-set, along with their purpose-based mission, this district has established a strong foundation for a high-performance culture. Their results attest to this fact. Whittier Union's five comprehensive high schools were ranked in the top third of all of California's schools with similar demographics. The district was one of only nine districts in the state to have more than one high school rank a 10 among similar schools. Additionally, three of the district's high schools made *Newsweek*'s America's Best High Schools List. Less than six percent of the nation's high schools made the list. The superintendent was quoted: "We will continue to set the bar high for all of our students and do 'Whatever It Takes' to help them reach those goals so that they may leave us well prepared for the challenges of college and beyond" (www.wuhsd.org).

VISION IN REDMOND SCHOOL DISTRICT, OREGON

Vickie Fleming, former superintendent of Redmond School District, Oregon, is another leader who understands mission and vision as the guiding force behind the work of a successful school district. She engineered a district mission and vision project known as the Redmond Educational Vision (REV): A Blueprint for Action. The development of this comprehensive vision project involved all stakeholders in imagining the future for students in Redmond and answering the question, Why do we exist? The Redmond vision is: "Leading for Success in the 21st Century." The mission is: "Ensure a rigorous and relevant education that develops productive citizens for a local and global economy" (www.redmond.k12.or.us). Like Whittier Union and the Coca-Cola

Company, REV explicitly details the shared beliefs, values, and commitments it expects from its people. An entire blueprint for action was developed around this work, which includes clear and urgent themes, student knowledge and skills, instructional core, programmatic focus, and stakeholder connections. A five-year strategic plan for 2007–2012 was also developed, with the mission serving as the guiding light. The results in Redmond are impressive, and the district was recognized by the state of Oregon for "closing the achievement gap" in elementary schools (www.redmond.k12.or.us).

VISION AT FRAZIER INTERNATIONAL MAGNET SCHOOL, CHICAGO

Colette Unger-Teasley, principal of Frazier International Magnet School in the heart of Chicago, is a leader who shares the commitment to keeping the purpose and mission of her school in the forefront of staff's, parents', students', and the broader community's consciousness. Frazier serves students in grades K–8, who come from some of the most challenging home environments one can imagine. Commonly, one can find groups of young men hanging out on street corners in front of buildings in the neighborhood, which are laden with graffiti and protected with barred windows.

Frazier International Magnet School is part of the Chicago Public School system and, as such, accepts all students through a random lottery process. There are no achievement requirements, no discipline requirements, and no attendance requirements. The only qualification or entry requirement is that the student be enrolled in the Chicago Public School system. The student population is a reflection of the community surrounding it, as well as from the far south side of Chicago. More than 90 percent of the students are minority and qualify for free or reduced-price lunches. This may seem like a tough place to work, with insurmountable challenges; but not so.

I had the pleasure of working with the Frazier team on-site and found the staff there to be inspired, committed, happy, and optimistic. The principal has instilled a sense of pride and purpose into the culture of the school. This team exudes a can-do spirit and is motivated to perform at the highest possible levels. Staff members are well positioned to tackle the challenges that come their way. At the present time, that challenge is the Common Core State Standards (CCSS) and next-generation assessments in 2014–2015. Although the CCSS present more rigorous expectations in reading, writing, speaking, listening, and mathematics, the Frazier team is confident they will rise to the new demands by adjusting their current teaching practices. Figure 1.1 depicts student results on the Illinois Standards Achievement Test (ISAT) from 2009 at Frazier International. Frazier has the distinction of being Chicago's first 90/90/90 school for two consecutive years. 90/90/90 Schools™ are those with 90 percent ethnic minority, 90 percent free or reduced-price lunch,

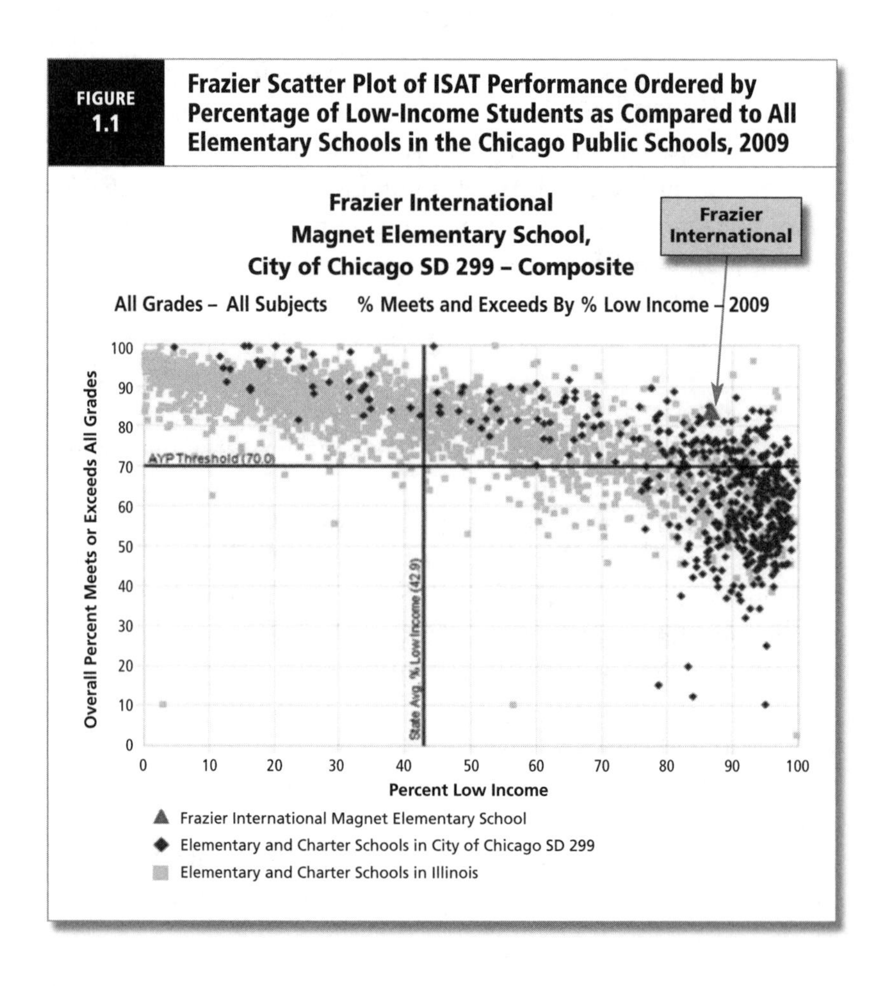

FIGURE 1.1 **Frazier Scatter Plot of ISAT Performance Ordered by Percentage of Low-Income Students as Compared to All Elementary Schools in the Chicago Public Schools, 2009**

and 90 percent proficiency on state assessments (Reeves, 2005). I will discuss the 90/90/90 Schools™ study in greater depth in Chapter Two.

During the 2009–2010 school year, 91.9 percent of the students met or exceeded Illinois State standards on the 2010 ISAT test, increasing their performance to 93.3 percent meeting or exceeding standards in 2010–2011. Frazier ranked 21 out of more than 500 elementary schools in Chicago, including selective enrollment, magnet, neighborhood, and charter schools. The governor of Illinois proclaimed a week in October 2010 as "Frazier International Beating the Odds and Educating Our Children Week" in Illinois.

Such successful results do not come without complete engagement and commitment to the collective purpose. The Frazier team demonstrates a strong collective efficacy and they believe they are making a real difference in the lives of the children and families they serve. Mrs. Unger-Teasley has successfully tapped into the intrinsic motivation in her team members and has achieved extraordinary results. The culture at Frazier is one of high performance, no excuses, focus, and excellence.

THE ROLE OF THE LEADER

How can all school principals establish a clear, purpose-based mission and vision for their schools, and what benefits will they reap? The good news is that people coming into education do so to make a difference in the life of a child. However, in order to create a culture centered on a purpose-driven mission, the principal must articulate it, celebrate it, and constantly communicate it to everyone touched by the school. Principals must engage their staffs in regular conversations about the mission of the school. They should constantly ask, Why do we exist? What are our hopes and dreams for our students? What actions can we take together to meet our goals? Is this the best we can be? School leaders must also listen to the thoughts, dreams, and visions of the people who work at the school and demonstrate how they are all connected.

Leaders must recognize this critical component of human motivation and move away from carrot-and-stick accountability plans. Give people a challenge; allow some autonomy for tackling the challenge; and support and give praise for effort, dedication, and working together. All of these forces will build a strong purpose culture and tap the intrinsic motivation that each human being brings to work.

A great exercise for any school faculty is to reflect on why they became teachers. At the next staff gathering, divide the group into small groups of three or four. Ask them to share the reasons they became teachers. Someone in each group should record the responses and then review them with group members. The group should identify and discuss the patterns or themes they see in their personal responses, and post them on large Post-it paper for a whole-faculty discussion. Ask the faculty to do a gallery walk to see the responses from every group and note the patterns and themes for all groups. Finally, lead the staff in a discussion about what they see they have in common, how their drives and desires as teachers align with the school's vision and mission. Again ask the question, Why do we exist? The answers will be on the wall.

Teachers will respond that they wanted to make difference, they wanted to pay back, they wanted to improve their community, and so on. The responses will not differ among grade levels, content areas, or geographic locations. It is the responsibility of the principal to take these responses, marry them with his own, and craft a mission and vision that answer the question, Why do we exist? But the work cannot stop here. As Drucker argues, the first task of the leader in a nonprofit organization is to ensure that everybody sees the mission, hears it, and lives it. The leader must use the mission as the filter for all decisions, all expenditures, and all communications.

A well-articulated, purpose-driven mission will focus the team on the right work. It will enable them to see the big picture. It will provide them a North Star that will guide them to unite for a purpose bigger than themselves, impossible to achieve alone. It will satisfy their desire for a challenge and their need to contribute to the greater good. It will serve as the vehicle for struggling schools to become high performing and propel high performers to greater levels of success. Most importantly, tapping the human drive for challenging, purpose-driven work will result in a culture of high performance. Leaders who invest the time to do this work well will have engaged teams who are prepared and eager to tackle the ever-increasing demands of educating America's children.

SUMMARY
KEY POINTS

- Human beings are driven to engage in work they find challenging, absorbing, and fulfilling.
- Human beings derive pleasure from solving a puzzle or conquering a challenge; in fact, they are intrinsically motivated to do so.
- Traditional methods of motivating workers with reward-and-punishment, carrot-and-stick, and if-then scenarios do little to motivate knowledge-based workers and could have the opposite of the intended effect.
- All organizations are capable of instilling a purpose motive by engaging people in frequent discussions and opportunities to share insights, goals, problems, and motivations.
- School leaders have the luxury of a built-in purpose motive and must capitalize on it.
- Serving the greater good of a school community is a basis for a purpose-driven mission and vision for schools.
- Schools with clear vision and purpose were found to be higher performing than those without.
- It is possible to achieve extraordinary results in the face of daunting challenges by uniting a school team around a strong purpose, motive, and vision.

CHAPTER TWO

HPC SECRET 2: A Few Vital Behaviors Can Change the World

Discover a few vital behaviors, change those, and problems—no matter their size— topple like a house of cards.

Patterson, Grenny, Maxfield, McMillan, and Switzler,
Influencer: The Power to Change Anything

THE CASE OF POSITIVE DEVIANTS

Creating a high-performance culture in schools is indeed a challenge, but is possible. We have the knowledge, research, examples of success, and resources essential to establish a performance culture in every school. What we lack is discipline, focus, and follow-through to implement a few vital behaviors that provide leverage toward becoming a performance culture. The fact that the literature shows us many and varied examples of schools beating the odds shows us it can be done. These schools, like Frazier International from Chapter One, are known as *positive deviants.* A closer look at the concept of positive deviants can help all schools become high performers.

The term "positive deviant" is a sort of contradiction in and of itself. How can something or someone be positive if they have deviant characteristics? Think of it this way: positive deviants are outliers. They deviate from the norm in a positive way. These outliers succeed against all odds. When we study positive deviants, we are looking for the common thread, a few vital behaviors, that set them apart from the pack. We focus on the successful exceptions, not the failing norm. According to the authors of *The Power of Positive Deviance*, the positive deviance problem-solving process teaches us to pay attention differently; to awaken our minds, which are accustomed to overlooking outliers; and to cultivate skepticism about the assumption "That's just the way it is." Once we grasp this concept, paying attention to observable exceptions draws us naturally to the "who," the "what," and especially the "how" (Pascale, Sternin, and Sternin, 2010, p. 3).

The process of positive deviance has been applied largely as a community improvement endeavor designed to help people in Third World countries ravaged by drought, famine, disease, and illiteracy. More recently, however, the process is being used in corporations and schools to address some of the most daunting and persistent problems. Along a spectrum of change tools, the positive deviance approach is one among many participatory methods. Its basic premise is that the solutions to some of our most challenging problems already exist and have already been found and used successfully by members of the community itself. These innovators, or positive deviants, have succeeded even though they share the same constraints, issues, and barriers as others who have not been successful (Pascale, Sternin, and Sternin, 2010, p. 4). In 2008, the *New York Times Magazine* touted positive deviance in its annual "Year in Ideas" and did so because the process had successfully altered the lives of millions of people around the world, including nations in Africa, Asia, and Latin America, and in the United States and Canada. What follow are a few examples of positive deviance in practice.

The Carter Center in Atlanta has devoted years to solving one of the most horrific and persistent health challenges affecting millions of people in Africa and Asia. Led by Dr. Donald Hopkins, the team has worked to eradicate the guinea worm parasite from remote villages by addressing unhealthy water-drinking habits. Hopkins and his team use the positive deviance approach to identify a few vital behaviors to drive the change process in these villages by teaching the inhabitants how to avoid suffering and spreading the scourge. When the villagers drink stagnant, unfiltered water, they take in the guinea worm larvae, which nest in the abdominal tissue. There the worms grow until reaching lengths as great as three feet. Eventually, the worms seek a way out of the human body by excreting an acid to make a path through the person's skin. As the worm approaches the surface of the skin, painful blisters emerge. The only relief for the infected is to soak the blistered area in water. Thus, they go to the same water source where they contracted the disease and the process starts all over. The exiting worm lays thousands of eggs in the water and the women scoop them up during their daily collection of water, bringing them back to the village in the drinking water. Sufferers of the disease are out of work for many weeks. Their work consists mainly of subsistence farming, and their affliction leads to untended crops and starvation. Children become sick and cannot attend school, and the cycles of poverty, illiteracy, and sickness continue, as they have for more than 3,500 years (Patterson, et al., 2007).

How did the positive deviance process help in this situation? Dr. Hopkins believed that if he could identify a few vital behaviors and share these with villages around the globe, he could eradicate the worm and save millions of people from suffering. First, the team went into villages in Asia and Africa that should have been affected by the disease, but somehow were not. They studied the disease-free villages, which had close neighbors with the same water source, but that were ravaged by the guinea worm. They zeroed in on water collection and transport in the worm-free villages and identified a few vital behaviors that made a huge difference in the health of the people. They noticed that the women in the disease-free outliers group used their skirts to filter the water from the river water pot into a second empty pot. In essence they filtered out the dangerous worm larvae. Eureka! The villagers had discovered their own solution to a problem that had plagued others for thousands of years. The team noted a few other vital behaviors and then shared them with villagers across the globe. The team has achieved what others have thought impossible. They have helped millions of people avoid this disease and found the vital behaviors necessary to do so right in the villages the disease affects. "Soon, Dr. Hopkins and his team will have laid claim to something never before accomplished in human history. They will have eradicated a global disease without finding a cure" (Patterson, et al., 2007, p. 17).

THE PROCESS OF POSITIVE DEVIANCE

While this achievement is incredible and wonderful, what does this have to do with the culture in a school? Let's examine the *process* of positive deviance and compare its characteristics to more widely known methods for educational improvement or change. The basic premise of positive deviance is that every community or organization has individuals who use unique and/or simple solutions to solve the most troublesome problems that their counterparts have not yet solved. Figure 2.1 illus-

FIGURE 2.1 A Comparison of Traditional Methods of Improvement or Change and Methods Favored in Positive Deviance

Rather than ...	In Positive Deviance ...
Import "best practices" from outside the organization.	People are identified who are doing well inside, and then those behaviors are vetted, analyzed, and tailored for use by members of other parts of the organization.
Having technical experts or managers tell frontline people what to do.	Frontline people learn to solve problems, co-discover, and teach each other.
Letting frontline people do whatever they want once the decision for higher participation has been made.	People are provided with boundaries so that the greater good of the community and the overarching needs of the organization are met. Through the promotion of widespread reflective practice, greater awareness and informed actions are made possible.
Hoping that people will follow through on commitments.	Accountability mechanisms (peer to peer and manager to direct report) are provided and organizational energy is generated that ensures promised items are followed up on.
Having people execute their daily tasks by rote.	People become more energized to *do* the work that they own and even *improve* it.

Source: Devane (2009).

trates the differences between the positive deviance process and traditional approaches for change and improvement.

The steps in positive deviance may seem simple and straightforward,

FIGURE 2.2 **Steps in the Process for Positive Deviance**

Define **the problem or the opportunity.**	Look for causes and current practices. Collect relevant data. This step is done by the leader or leadership team.
Define **the outcome you are looking for.**	Without a clear end in mind, it will be difficult to design specific activities and vital behaviors. This step is done by the leaders.
Determine **the outliers, or those who are getting the desired results under the same conditions as those who are not.**	This step is done by the group seeking improvement, and is based on dialogue.
Discover **their uncommon practices and behaviors that enable them to outperform others with the same challenges.**	This step is done by the local group seeking improvement and is based on dialogue and discovery by that group.
Design **and implement interventions that enable others in the organization to access and practice the vital behaviors.**	The focus here is on the doing aspect rather than the transfer of knowledge. This step is done by the local improvement group based on dialogue and discovery.
Discern **if the vital behaviors and practices are working.**	Monitor and evaluate results and compare to the data collected in Step 1. This step is done by the local improvement group and is based on dialogue and discovery.
Disseminate **findings and the positive deviance process to other needed locations in the organization.**	The findings should be vetted for relevance in conversations with stakeholders. The process of identifying local positive deviance would be introduced for developing other solutions beyond the initial findings for a particular target area. This is done by the leadership team using dialogue and training.

Source: Devane (2009).

but they actually require a shift in thinking, and that does not happen overnight. We have to shift our thinking from knowledge being the change driver to behavior being the change driver. We have to shift from the leader directing the work of others to the leader as inquirer and facilitator. We have to become comfortable shifting from knowing the answers at the start of a change to discovering answers along the way and adjusting appropriately. Figure 2.2 illustrates the steps in the process.

POSITIVE DEVIANCE IN SCHOOLS

You may recognize some of the positive deviance process steps from the inquiry cycles you currently use in your organization. The Data Teams process from The Leadership and Learning Center very closely resembles this process, with the focus on identifying and replicating best practices, or behaviors, that are working. Data Teams seek to identify the outliers in an effort to bring vital behaviors into the light for all team members to see and practice. In essence, we look for the invisible in plain sight!

One high school in California has taken the positive deviance approach to analyzing and solving their dropout problem. Merced High School graduates only 50 percent of its incoming freshman class, which is lower than the national average and the lowest in the Merced Union High School District (Po, 2011). Merced is a very diverse school of 2,700 students, more than 50 percent of whom are Hispanic, 20 percent white, 20 percent Asian, and less than 10 percent African American. African American and Latino students are more likely to drop out, as well as the Hmong and Vietnamese girls (Po, 2011). A teacher at the school applied for a grant from the Positive Deviance Initiative at Tufts University in Boston and started using the program to identify the outliers.

Each year, the teacher and her team flag students as "at risk" or "positives." The hypothesis is that by putting students, the "positives," in groups with the "at-risk," the "positives'" successful behaviors can be learned by those that need them, the "at-risk." The "positives" live in the same neighborhoods, face the same challenges, such as gangs, drugs, sex, and other high-risk behaviors. Yet they do their homework, earn good grades, and aspire to go to college. During the 2009–2010 school year, the groups organized and met twice a month. Participation is now up to 70 students and several success stories have emerged. Time is needed to collect more data and provide more time for students in the "at risk" group to adopt the vital behaviors they learn from their successful counterparts. The staff members at the school are very encouraged by the results to date (Po, 2011).

In another example highlighted by Collins and Hansen in *Great by Choice: Uncertainty, Chaos, and Luck—Why Some Thrive Despite Them All*, the former president of Arizona State University, and chairman of the Center for the Future of Arizona, Lattie Coor, expressed an interest in improving the education of Latino children across the state. In fact, he saw this challenge as one of the top priorities for the state of Arizona. He contacted Collins because he wanted to use the "matched pair" process used by Collins to identify great organizations and apply it to identifying schools that were great at serving Latino children. This process easily compares to the process of positive deviance. Coor's team of researchers was responsible for the *Beat the Odds* study, which resulted in several very interesting findings. The team discovered that the schools who beat the odds with Latino children focused on the barriers that they had control over. These schools held themselves accountable, independent of any external accountability measures, for increasing achievement for all students. They established a clear bottom line of acceptable academic performance, and they worked toward that goal with constant focus, strategic action, and consistent data analysis. They did not blame families, students, or economics for poor performance. Rather they looked squarely at student performance issues and took responsibility for them. They did not look for an external "silver bullet" to solve their student achievement challenges. If students were not learning, they looked within to find the reasons, and they made changes to the school. And they refused to let any student lag behind. If any one student was not learning, then the school was not doing its job.

The research team also found that factors often cited by principals and teachers alike as barriers to student achievement did not distinguish the higher-performing schools from their comparison lower-performing schools. These factors included class size, length of the school day, lack of funding, and the degree of parental involvement.

The high performers did not focus on these factors as barriers. They recognized that these factors were not within their control and therefore they did not spend time discussing, debating, or considering them. Again, the highly successful outliers, the successful exceptions, if you will, focused only on the factors within their control.

One of the success schools identified in the study was Alice Byrne Elementary School in Yuma, Arizona. This school emerged as a positive deviant in the study because it faced very tough challenges with the high enrollment and low socioeconomic status of its Latino students, and yet the school increased the students' reading achievement by 20 percentage points, beating the state averages. The principal at the school, Julie Tate Peach, attributed their success to a few vital behaviors of her staff, behaviors that were followed consistently and effectively throughout their successful turnaround. The vital behaviors included constant monitoring of student achievement data, followed by corrective action by every staff member. Peach created a collaborative culture of teachers and administrators who worked side by side poring over the data and making decisions for each student to achieve. This cycle was described as "never-ending" instruction, assessment, intervention, kid-by-kid, in a relentless march until the end of the year. Improving results increased the teachers' confidence and motivation, which increased their focus and discipline, which then drove improved results (Collins and Hansen, p. 97).

The results of this study, to identify the positive deviant schools in educating Latino children, were shared at a statewide principals meeting. The study was not called a positive deviance study, nor were the steps of positive deviance explicitly followed, but the premises were exactly the same:

- Look at all of the Arizona schools working to educate high numbers of Latino children.
- Find the ones who are doing well and study them in comparison to like schools who are not doing well.
- Identify the vital behaviors in the successful exceptions, or positive deviants, and share the results with others who continue to struggle with the same challenges.

Thus, following the process of positive deviance helped others learn the vital behaviors and more effectively educate Latino children in their schools.

The concept of positive deviance is slowly creeping into education but is not yet widely used in educational circles. Dennis Sparks argues that "amplifying positive deviance is a promising, nonprescriptive approach for schools that see value in this premise and are ready to empower teachers through its inquiry process" (Sparks, 2004, p. 188). Although not specifically using the steps in positive deviance, educational researchers have mined data over the past decade to find exactly the type of outliers that users of positive deviance look for. In works by Karin Chenoweth at Education Trust, Heather Zavadsky at the National Center for Educational Accountability and the Broad Foundation, and Douglas Reeves and colleagues at The Leadership and Learning Center, the positive deviants are well documented and the vital behaviors cataloged in detail. Each of these researchers identified positive deviant schools that are outperforming their counterparts with the same challenges. These successful schools implement a few vital behaviors consistently and relentlessly to solve their most pressing problems.

THE 90/90/90 SCHOOLS™

One of the studies conducted over a decade ago by Dr. Douglas Reeves found the outliers and identified the vital behaviors as chronicled in *Accountability in Action: A Blueprint for Learning Organizations.* The 90/90/90 Schools™ research, as it was known, identified high-poverty, high-minority, and high-performing schools. Since this was such an anomaly at the time, and to a great extent is true today, the study sent shock waves through the education community. Schools with 90 percent of students on free or reduced-price lunch, 90 percent ethnic minority, and 90 percent proficiency on state or national tests were indeed outliers. Schools and districts interested in serving their underperforming students welcomed this research, while those sticking to the bell curve met these findings with skepticism and doubt.

What were the vital behaviors in these high-performing schools that caused them to overcome the barriers to success that hindered so many schools with the same demographic factors? According to Reeves, "... we sought to identify the extent to which there was a common set of behaviors exhibited by the leaders and teachers in schools with high achievement, high minority enrollment, and high poverty levels" (Reeves, 2005, p. 187). As a result, the original study identified five common vital behaviors, which include:

- A laser focus on student achievement
- Clear curriculum choices
- Frequent assessments and multiple opportunities for improvement
- An emphasis on nonfiction writing
- Collaborative scoring of student work

In the decade since the study, these findings have been validated in additional research and do not seem so progressive in 2011. However, 10 years ago, it was not common to walk into schools and see data charts and graphs posted in faculty rooms and principals' offices. It was not common to observe teachers working together in the relentless pursuit of high achievement for every student. Giving struggling students multiple opportunities for success on formative assessments was not accepted practice, nor was it common to hear conversations about all students learning power standards in reading, writing, and mathematics.

The typical course of action in high-poverty, high-minority schools was to blame low achievement on families, home conditions, language barriers, and the students themselves. Most schools with these challenges existed in a culture of low expectations. The prevailing attitude in 1999 was that low achievement in high-poverty, high-minority schools was "just the way things are," and there was nothing teachers or administrators could do to improve things. Since the identification of the vital behaviors of the 90/90/90 Schools™ and the subsequent validation of these findings in other research by James Popham, John Hattie, and Robert Marzano, more schools are adopting the vital behaviors from the 90/90/90 Schools™, as well as identifying their own outliers and maximizing the solutions they find through on-site action research.

Wayne Township Metropolitan School Corporation, located in

Indianapolis, Indiana, is a district that demonstrated academic improvement with high-minority, high-poverty students by using the findings from the 90/90/90 Schools™ and by finding and learning from their own outliers, or positive deviants. Facing the challenges of high poverty rates, increasing numbers of English Language Learners speaking more than twenty-five different languages, and high minority enrollments, the district has beat the odds and has shown strong improvement applying a few vital behaviors. They began with a focus and full implementation of nonfiction writing at every level and an absolute focus on collaboration in every school (Reeves, 2005). Interestingly, by 2002 the schools with the highest poverty levels made the greatest gains because those schools displayed the most intense focus on the vital behaviors. These gains exceeded 20 percent in several schools within the district. Reeves concluded,

> While no one disputes that poverty, linguistic differences, and culture can be important variables influencing student achievement, the research is clear that variables in teaching, curriculum, and leadership are profoundly important. In fact, these variables, that teachers and leaders can control, are more influential over student achievement than the intractable variables of poverty, culture, and language. (Reeves, 2005, p. 204)

KNOWING VERSUS DOING

Even though the literature on many outliers, such as Frazier International and schools in Wayne Township, has been widely distributed, and access to the information is available with only a few keystrokes on a computer, many school leaders have not acted upon the information in a way that will make a difference for the schools and students they serve. We continue to have an implementation gap, or as Jeffrey Pfeffer and Robert Sutton would say, a "knowing-doing gap." Leaders and teachers have a great deal of knowledge on how to improve performance, but instead act in contradiction to their instincts or the data available to them. How do you know you have a knowing-doing gap in your school or district? Consider these points:

- Talking a lot is mistaken for doing a lot.
- There is a belief that managers are people who talk and others do.
- People are evaluated on how smart they sound, rather than on what they do.
- No follow-up is done to ensure that what was said is actually done.

(Pfeffer and Sutton, 2000, p. 54)

The focus here is on the *doing*, not talking about doing. A few vital behaviors are what make a difference in the success of solving a challenge. Reeves cautions schools about developing weighty strategic plans that contain many strategies. These plans sometimes contain 50, 60, 100 or more strategies and are organized in three-ring binders with tabs, table of contents, appendices, and the like. "Complex organizations that create meaningful change in a short period of time are not weighted down by voluminous strategic plans; they have absolute clarity about a few things that must be done immediately" (Reeves, 2005, p. 204). Meeting, talking, and creating complex strategic plans may be necessary, but the consistent implementation of a few vital behaviors is what drives change.

Principals, central office administrators, teacher grade-level teams, and content departments can apply this "secret" immediately to their work. Get a team together to examine the most recent student achievement data and identify the outliers, or positive deviants. Engage the team in a discussion about the results and develop a process for identifying the vital behaviors of the outliers. Remember, an outlier faces the same challenges and barriers to success as his or her counterparts, but shows remarkable success, while the others continue to struggle. The answers to your most pressing problem may be hiding from you in plain sight. The process works best when the community itself discovers its own vital behaviors, so it is critical that teachers, who will be affected by any changes in practice, be involved in the process to identify the positive deviants.

SUMMARY
KEY POINTS

- The consistent implementation of a few vital behaviors can bring us the change we desire.
- Creating a high-performance culture involves identifying the vital behaviors from within and outside the organization and following through on their implementation.
- The concept of positive deviants, the outliers who defy the odds and achieve in the face of formidable challenges, provides us with the knowledge and confidence that all challenges can be overcome.
- The premise of positive deviance is that solutions to the most pressing challenges can be found by looking for the outliers and zeroing in on a few vital behaviors that set them apart from the low performers.
- The 90/90/90 Schools™ research uncovered schools that were positive deviants as they overcame the challenges of high poverty, high minority, and low achievement and instead achieved 90 percent proficiency rates.
- The vital behaviors of these schools included:
  - –A laser focus on student achievement
  - –Clear curriculum choices
  - –Frequent assessments and multiple opportunities for success
  - –Schoolwide emphasis on nonfiction writing
  - –Collaborative scoring of student work
- The process of positive deviance involves:
  - –Defining the problem and the outcome
  - –Determining the outliers
  - –Discovering the uncommon behaviors
  - –Designing and implementing strategies that allow others in the organization to access and learn the behaviors
  - –Discerning if the vital behaviors are working
  - –Disseminating the findings and expanding the process

CHAPTER THREE

HPC SECRET 3: Cooperation and Collaboration Are Part of Human Evolution

Evolutionary biologists and psychologists have found neural and, possibly, genetic evidence of a human predisposition to cooperate. These findings suggest that instead of using controls or carrots and sticks to motivate people, companies should use systems that rely on engagement and a sense of common purpose.

Yochai Benkler, "The Unselfish Gene,"
Harvard Business Review

THE SCIENCE OF SELFISHNESS

For many years now, leaders in all professions have been taught that human beings are naturally selfish creatures. In 1976, Richard Dawkins wrote *The Selfish Gene,* which suggested that in order to get workers to cooperate with one another toward a common purpose or goal, altruism and generosity would have to be explicitly taught, because human beings were biologically selfish individuals (Benkler, 2011). Selfishness was considered just part of the human DNA. For the next 30 or so years, leaders of organizations grounded their work on the notion that all workers were naturally self-interested and would ask, What's in it for me? If the leadership could not clearly demonstrate how work would benefit individuals concerned only with their material gain, then the effort would die a quick death.

This theory of self-interest above everything else has continued until recent research from the fields of psychology, sociology, political science, experimental economics, and evolutionary biology has proved otherwise. In 2006, Harvard University mathematical biologist Martin Nowak published an article in *Science* magazine that offered "natural cooperation" in a competitive world as a possible third fundamental principle of evolution, along with mutation and natural selection. According Yochai Benkler, Professor for Entrepreneurial Legal Studies at Harvard University and author of "The Unselfish Gene," published in The *Harvard Business Review,* and *The Penguin and the Leviathan: How Cooperation Triumphs over Self-Interest*:

> Through the work of many scientists, we have begun to see evidence across several disciplines that people are in fact more cooperative and selfless—or behave far less selfishly—than we have assumed. Perhaps humankind is not so inherently selfish after all.
>
> Evolutionary biologists and psychologists have found neural and, possibly, genetic evidence of a human predisposition to cooperate. These findings suggest that instead of using controls or carrots and sticks to motivate people, companies should use systems that rely on engagement and a sense of common purpose. (Benkler, 2011, p. 79)

COLLABORATIVE SCHOOL CULTURES

If we take the scientific research on cooperation to heart and compare it to the changes or evolution seen in schools over the past 10 years, we know that the arguments by Benkler have merit. Schools that are meeting and exceeding the challenges they face are doing so by creating cultures that value cooperation, collaboration, and teamwork. Reeves asserts, "... solitary efforts were of little benefit to our Cro-Magnon predecessors, and they are not the source of our successes today. We survive as a species and as leaders of organizations not due to solitary efforts but due to organizational and collaborative success" (Reeves, 2006, p. 26).

Schools have made progress in abandoning the traditional image of the classroom teacher being a lone ranger in her room with the door closed and doing her own thing. We have worked hard to recognize that human beings accomplish more together than alone, and human beings are naturally social and *need* to connect with others. Fullan suggests that when people work in conjunction with other practitioners, they also become more socially engaged. Such work is cognitively and socially more intrinsically rewarding, and more effective for addressing the problems at hand (Fullan, 2011, p. 21).

In fact, "Neuroscience shows that a reward circuit is triggered in our brains when we cooperate with one another, and that provides a scientific basis that at least some people want to cooperate given the choice because it feels good" (Benkler, 2011, p. 82). Norman Doidge (2007) asserts that the brain can grow and change itself given the proper nourishment. The nourishment for the brain includes the need for social interaction and cooperation. The *ability* to cooperate and collaborate, however, is not part of the human DNA. The "natural cooperation" as a third fundamental principle of evolution suggested by Nowak earlier in this chapter may well be true, but the ability to do it well in a professional setting may not come naturally. If we are to survive on this shrinking planet, we must, all of us, develop skills for effective and meaningful cooperation and collaboration.

The same holds true for schools if they are to endure and thrive as an institution. According to Rick DuFour, "Teacher isolation is so deeply ingrained in the traditional fabric of schools that leaders cannot simply invite teachers to create a collaborative culture. They must identify and implement specific, strategic interventions that help teachers work together rather than alone" (quoted by Dennis Sparks, 2004, p. 111). This might be a tall order for principals, given that they typically observe instruction one classroom at a time, share feedback one teacher at a time, and focus on the improvement of instruction one-on-one with each teacher. In essence, they work to strengthen the *individual* growth of teachers, and not so much attention has been given to the collective growth of the staff.

CREATING A COLLABORATIVE CULTURE

This scenario is changing, as more attention and priority is being given to professional learning that occurs through the daily interactions of teachers when they cooperatively plan lessons, analyze student data, and solve problems together for the benefit of an entire grade level or content team. Many schools are striving to create collaborative cultures through the use of professional learning communities and Data Teams. "Because culture is the sum total of the beliefs of community members and their interactions, creating such a culture means establishing norms and practices that lead to trust and mutual respect, continuous improvement, team-focused collaboration, clarity of thought, candid expressions of views, and interpersonal accountability for the fulfillment of commitments" (Sparks, 2004, p. 113). Attention to these factors by school leaders is a must if they hope to create a true professional learning community grounded in cooperation and collaboration. Failure to set clear expectations will result in schools who say they have professional learning communities, but where nothing has changed in the culture and they are void of teams that effectively cooperate and collaborate.

High-performing cooperative teams have quality connections to each other. They share common goals and purpose, they trust the intentions of each other, and they are highly engaged in the work. These individuals do not ask, What's in it for me? as described in *The Selfish Gene.* Rather, they are energized by the work and see the fruits of their labor and successful cooperation as a contribution to the greater good. They feel part of creating something bigger than themselves and something they could not have achieved alone. Benkler argues that "systems that harness intrinsic motivation and self-directed cooperative behavior don't need to limit themselves to knowledge of what people will do. Engaged workers become monitors of their own actions and engage enthusiastically in the work" (Benkler, 2011, p. 80).

Paul Adler, Charles Heckscher, and Laurence Prusak, professors of management and organization at the University of Southern California, Rutgers University, and Columbia University, respectively, suggest that organizations must master a set of new skills in order to build collaborative cultures. They believe a new form of organization is emerging that is innovative and efficient, agile and scalable, and maintains a focus on knowledge production (Adler, Heckscher, and Prusak, 2011, p. 97). These researchers' conclusions about the emergence of a new form of organization have great applicability to school organizations. Schools must be both innovative and efficient. They must be agile and scalable. But most importantly, they must be focused on knowledge production for students and staff alike. Many schools already demonstrate a number of the organizational skills that the researchers include on their essentials list. The four skills essential to building collaborative communities are:

- Defining and building a shared purpose
- Cultivating an ethic of contribution
- Developing processes that enable people to work together in flexible but disciplined projects
- Creating an infrastructure in which collaboration is valued and rewarded

(Adler, Heckscher, and Prusak, 2011, p. 96).

Collaborative Culture at the SEED School

The SEED School in Washington, D.C., is an example of this kind of bone-deep collaboration and cooperation. Led by Head of School Charles Adams and Principal Kara Stacks, the team works to ensure the college acceptance of each and every student in the school. SEED was showcased in the film *Waiting for Superman* and was a feature story on the *60 Minutes* television show. SEED was the nation's first urban public boarding school and remains one of two in existence in the United States. Located in the heart of Ward 7 in Washington, D.C., the school strives to serve students who live in the neighborhood. Although a charter school, SEED serves Washington, D.C., public school students and accepts those who apply through a lottery system. Once the seats are taken, the students go onto a waiting list. There are no academic requirements for entry, and no student is turned away if they are enrolled in the D.C. public schools, and they are selected through the random lottery process. The overwhelming majority of SEED students are African American and from neighborhoods that struggle economically. The primary mission of the SEED School is to provide an outstanding, intensive educational program that prepares children, both academically and socially, for success in college. To that end, SEED sent 95 percent of their 2011 senior class to a four-year college or university, and trends show that an average of 59 percent of them will complete a four-year degree. Eighty-two percent of SEED's students will be first-generation college students (www.seedschooldc.org).

I learned firsthand about this remarkable school while working with them on-site to implement the Common Core State Standards. What I noticed immediately is that both students and staff are congenial and welcoming to each other as well as visitors, and they share a high degree of collegiality. But more importantly, they demonstrated very strong cooperative and collaborative skills. The culture of this school is one of high performance. They have a purpose-driven mission and they work cooperatively to achieve it. The principal has high expectations for both the students and the staff at SEED, and she understands that a high level of support and coaching is required to sustain this no-excuses, all-students-to-college conviction. During a meeting with the leadership team, which included the assistant principal, literacy coach, and numerous teachers, Principal Stacks modeled the level of cooperation and collaboration she expects from her staff. She did not speak first or most often. She did not direct others' thinking. She did not make mandates. Rather, she frequently asked the team to respond to questions and probes to deepen her understanding of their thoughts.

We developed a plan to move forward that represented the best thinking by the group. It was not the principal's plan. It was a plan reflecting what the team believed was best for the school and the staff. They demonstrate what Adler and colleagues call the *ethic of contribution.* It exists in a culture where people who look beyond their specific roles and advance the common purpose are the most valued in the organization. It was clear that team members were accustomed to speaking freely, and that norms of professional conduct had been established. The purpose at SEED is ingrained in the work. All students will achieve at grade level, and extraordinary effort will be made to get them there, regardless of how low they are when they enter the school in the sixth grade. All students will go to college and be prepared well by the SEED School.

Reeves makes a distinction between congeniality, collegiality, and collaboration (Reeves, 2009). While he asserts that the first two are essential for strong social interactions and personal connections to the school, they are not as difficult nor do they have as much impact as effective collaboration. In order for professional collaboration to become part of the school culture, staff members must be provided time, practice, and feedback to improve their work. Just like learning anything new, at first the task is uncomfortable. It's like learning to ride a bicycle. Very few of us just jumped on a bike and started riding successfully. We needed training wheels, we needed support as the training wheels were removed, and then, one day, our support was standing behind us as we rode down the street. Our supporters (usually our parents) were left yelling behind us, You are doing it! You are riding by yourself! Learning effective collaboration skills in a professional setting, like learning to ride a bike, takes time, practice, support, and feedback. One day, we will be highly functioning, but it will not come without deliberate effort and support from school leaders and coaches. It is the leader's responsibility to take notice of the work and provide evidence of progress. This will help sustain the effort on collaboration and further motivate the team to stick with it.

This kind of cooperation and collaboration is more important now than ever. With the rising demands from the private sector on the quality of schools and the adoption of the Common Core State Standards by 45 states and Washington, D.C., to date, teamwork and collaboration is the only way to meet these growing challenges. It will be incumbent on school leaders at all levels to model the way by demonstrating strong cooperative and collaborative skills, just as Kara Stacks has done at the SEED School. The modeling of cooperation and collaboration from the boardroom to the classroom will send a strong message about what is expected and valued by the organization. In cases where superintendents and senior administrators exhort the values of collaboration and then behave as isolationists and engage in turf battles, the damage can be significant. Teachers and principals will develop a cynical view of their leaders and the importance of what they say, and they will likely lessen their commitment to the efforts around collaborating and cooperating with others.

COLLABORATION AND THE COMMON CORE STATE STANDARDS

This issue of genuine collaboration becomes even more important as we prepare to implement the CCSS in grades K–12 in speaking, listening, reading, writing, and language. The standards explicitly require students to participate in collaborations with peers and make arguments supported with evidence and reasons. In fact, College and Career Readiness (CCR) Anchor Standard 1 for Speaking and Listening requires high school graduates to

> Prepare for and participate effectively in a range of conversations and collaborations with diverse partners, building on others' ideas and expressing their own clearly and persuasively. (www.corestandards.org)

When we drill down to the specific grade-level standards for CCR Anchor Standard 1 in speaking and listening, we find that very young students, including those in kindergarten, are expected to participate in collaborative discussions about grade-level topics with peers and adults, in large and smaller groups. They are expected to follow agreed-upon rules for discussions, such as listening to others and taking turns speaking (www.corestandards.org).

As students complete the third grade, the standards require that they

- Come to discussions prepared, having read or studied required material; explicitly draw on that preparation to explore ideas . . .
- Follow rules for discussion and gain the floor in

respectful ways, listen to others with care, and speak one at a time.

- Ask questions to check for understanding of information presented, stay on topic, and link their comments to the remarks of others.

(www.corestandards.org)

If you think back to some of the discussions you have had recently, has your team met the third-grade standards listed here for collaborations and discussions?

Indeed, the art and skill of effective cooperation and collaboration are what all humans strive for as we evolve as a species. As Fullan describes, "the ability to collaborate—on both a large and small scale—is one of the core requisites of post-modern society . . . [I]n short, without collaborative skills and relationships it is not possible to learn and to continue to learn as much as you need in order to be an agent for social improvement" (Fullan, 1993, pp. 17–18). It is personally satisfying and rewarding to solve a complex problem or conquer a challenge with a team of committed individuals. The emotional side of the human equation cannot be removed in the workplace. If leaders will recognize this aspect of human nature and capitalize on it, they will lay the foundation for becoming a high-performance culture. As Benkler concludes, "we need people who aren't focused only on payoffs, but do the best they can to learn, adapt, improve, and deliver results for the organization. Being internally motivated to bring these qualities to bear in a world where insight, creativity, and innovation can come from anyone, anytime, anywhere is more important than being able to calculate the costs, benefits and rewards . . ." (Benkler, 2011, p. 85).

SUMMARY
KEY POINTS

- Human beings are not the selfish individuals biologists once thought they were.
- Scientists are now reporting that humans have a predisposition to cooperate, and advances in neuroscience show that a reward circuit is triggered in our brains when we cooperate with one another.
- The ability to effectively cooperate and collaborate in a professional setting must be developed by communicating and following norms, establishing a common purpose, defining the intended outcomes, providing time to practice, and giving feedback on progress.
- Collaboration is different from congeniality and collegiality, and it is much more difficult to achieve and has a greater impact on the culture.
- Leaders must model the way if they expect teachers to learn effective cooperative and collaborative skills.
- The Common Core Standards require that students in kindergarten through high school demonstrate a distinct and complex set of collaborative skills.
- All school system staff, from the boardroom to the classroom, must provide examples and models for staff and students to follow as they work to master the skills required of them.
- Effective cooperation and collaboration means people look beyond their individual interests and instead focus on the interests of the organization as a whole.
- It is the leader's responsibility to communicate that these people are the most valued in the organization.

PART TWO

The *Simple Truths* to Creating a High-Performance School Culture

CHAPTER FOUR

HPC SIMPLE TRUTH 1: Teaching Talent Makes the Difference

Teachers are among the most powerful influences on learning.

John Hattie, *Visible Learning*

Now that the secrets that impact organizational culture have been revealed, an emphasis or review of the simple truths that impact school culture must follow. As stated in the introduction, these truths are not earth-shattering. They are not new, nor are they surprising. In fact, these simple truths are well known and accepted by school leaders as facts or rules to live by. However, it is startling how many leaders ignore the simple truths and forge ahead with practices they know are in stark contradiction to the simple truths of leading a high-performing school. Readers will recognize the simple truths that follow and gain new insights as to why they are the simple truths to live by in schools.

GREAT TEACHING

Great teachers get great results. We have all known teachers who succeed with all students no matter what the challenge. It makes no difference from year to year which students are on the roll, these teachers find a way to reach and teach each one of them. There is no argument that consistent quality instructional practices make a significant impact on student learning; in fact, they can be more powerful than the impact of poverty or home demographics. The good news is that teaching talent can be developed. *Talent* is not the result of a good gene pool or luck. In fact, teaching talent is the outcome of good instruction, support, feedback, and deliberate practice. Modern research in education has revealed that what teachers *do* rather than what they know makes the biggest difference in student learning. John Hattie, author of *Visible Learning: A Synthesis of Over 800 Meta-Analyses Relating to Achievement,* provides us with an outstanding source of research on the factors that have the greatest impact on student learning. This work took 15 years to compile and involved millions of students. The behaviors of talented teachers who make a statistical difference in the learning of the students can now be discerned in Hattie's work.

Hattie determined the influences that make the biggest difference in student learning outcomes by using effect sizes. According to Hattie, "an effect size provides a common expression of the magnitude of study outcomes for many types of outcome variables, such as school achievement" (Hattie, 2009, p. 7). Hattie submits that teachers can typically attain an increase in effect size of between 0.20 and 0.40 in student learning over the course of one school year. In order to achieve higher-than-average growth in one school year, teachers should be seeking effect sizes greater than 0.40, which would equal more than one year's growth in one year's time. In order to attain gains that are determined as excellent—that is, two to three years' growth in one year's time—they should be seeking effect sizes greater than 0.60. Hattie set his standard at 0.40, called the "zone of desired effects," to assist educators in identifying the influences that would garner above-average gains in student learning. Additionally, Hattie reports an effect size of 0.40 enables the influences to make real-world differences in student learning. Among the various influences on student learning in Hattie's research—the home, the curriculum, and the school—he found the influences of the teacher to be very powerful.

Over the past 20 years educators have considered teaching as both an art and a science. Hattie does not discount that, however the focus in his work is simply, "What makes a significant difference in achievement gains?" The act of teaching boils down to a change in student cognition. Therefore, it is critical for a teacher to know the intentions of the lesson, understand the understandings of each student in relation to those intentions, use that understanding to design challenging and meaningful progressions for learning, and know when the student has attained those intentions. All of this must be done in a safe environment for learning, established and maintained by the teacher, where error is expected and welcomed.

Interestingly, Hattie also addresses the impact of passion for both teachers and learners. He states that passion reflects the thrills and the frustrations of learning. It can be infectious and learned. It can and should be modeled by teachers. Learning new things can be a thrill for learners and a thrill for teachers, as they engage students in learning by fostering deliberate practice to attain understanding. Hattie acknowledges that he did not include studies on passion in his seminal work, mostly because it is rarely studied. However, he recognizes the influence that passion has on outcomes.

> It [passion] requires more than content knowledge, acts of skilled teaching, or engaged students to make the difference. It requires a love of the content, an ethical caring stance to wish to imbue others with a liking or even a love of the discipline being taught, and a demonstration that the teacher is not only teaching but learning—typically about the students' processes and outcomes of learning. (Hattie, 2009, p. 24)

It is clear from Hattie's research that variance in teacher effectiveness accounts for a significant percentage of the variance in student achievement. Hattie equates the difference to a 0.32 effect size. The variance in teacher quality is much more prominent in urban centers and lower socioeconomic schools, which is precisely where highly effective teachers are needed most.

Effective Teacher Behaviors

According to Hattie's research, the top three contributions from the teacher that have the greatest impact on student outcomes appear below. Note the effect sizes of these behaviors on student learning gains. All three of these contributions fall into Hattie's excellent range and will result in learning gains of two to three years in one year's time.

• *Microteaching (0.88 effect size)*

Microteaching typically takes place in a laboratory environment, where teachers in training or veteran teachers desirous of improving, conduct minilessons with students before a group of other teachers in order to engage in post-discussion about lesson effectiveness. In some cases, teachers are videotaped and the post-discussion occurs when the tape is viewed with colleagues. This type of teacher development puts professional practice under the microscope for deep analysis and decision making about continued improvement for teachers. It is the rich dialogue and exchange of teaching knowledge that makes this type of professional learning so substantial.

• *Teacher clarity (0.75 effect size)*

The teacher is clear as to the learning intentions for the lessons and the students are clear as to the expectations for success. During the lesson, clarity involved organization, explanations, examples, guided practice, and assessment of student learning as defined by Fendick (1990). The teacher's clarity of speech was also important and served as a prerequisite of teacher clarity.

• *Teacher-student relationships (0.72 effective size)*

In classes where the teacher has established strong relationships with students, student outcomes improve. It takes skill to develop the kind of productive relationships needed for improved student learning. These skills include listening, empathy, caring, and positive regard for others. Teachers can facilitate student development by showing their concern for each student's learning, as well as working to understand their perspective and provide them with feedback to allow them to self-assess. Teachers with positive relationships establish safe learning environments where the learning of all students is cherished, and the teacher serves as a change agent to move all students to higher levels of performance.

It is essential that skilled and promising teachers occupy every classroom if the United States is to achieve the goal of all students being college and career ready as stated in the Common Core State Standards. But this simple truth seems to escape so many superintendents and central office administrators. Most districts do not have an effective plan for managing human capital with the aim of developing teacher talent as a district priority. They have plans for recruitment and retention, but the strategies in these plans are the same ones from years ago and based on an old reality. Good teachers seek work in high-performance cultures, where all students are expected to achieve at high levels, and all teachers and administrators focus on effective teaching as the core function of the school. Effective teachers, like the ones described by Hattie, require cultures that value learning for all and provide quality professional development experiences. The level of skill and passion described in the research above can be attained by teachers if they are provided the right culture with quality development and opportunities to explore and learn from mistakes.

THE SHRINKING TALENT POOL

Unfortunately, far too few teachers find work in such environments, which contributes to the loss of millions of teachers to retirement and new teacher attrition at the entry level. In fact, we are at a critical juncture with the teaching force in this country. We currently have 1.8 million baby boomers in the classroom. We are expected to lose 1.5 million of them in the next eight years. Added to this is the annual loss of 2.5 million teachers of all ages due to job dissatisfaction. Sadly, American schools are increasingly without great teaching talent at a time when it is needed more than ever. Statistics show that young teachers are 184 percent more likely to leave the profession than middle-age teachers, and the attrition rate for teachers with one to three years of teaching experience has risen to 40 percent. The annual cost of this constant teacher churn exceeds $7 billion and shows no end in sight (National Commission on Teaching and America's Future, 2010). Recent cutbacks and layoffs have done little to stem the tide; if anything, the desperate public budgets have accelerated retirements and resignations.

Ultimately, every district in the nation will be affected by the shrinking pool of qualified teachers, and the competition for good teachers is in full swing. Principals and central offices must act now to ensure that all students will have quality teachers. Contrary to the past practice of just recruiting new people to replace the old, they must concentrate their efforts on developing teaching talent in the staff they have and retaining those teachers who show promise. High-performing schools have been doing this for years, and forward-thinking principals are well positioned to meet the expectations of the CCSS and new accountability measures coming in the form of next-generation assessments in 2014–2015. The rest will need to transform quickly in order to have any hope of meeting the new demands and realizing success toward their mission.

Human capital management is not a required course in any graduate program that prepares school principals. Therefore, we must look to the research in organizational effectiveness, successful schools, and the private sector to learn strategies and structures to manage human capital effectively. Many successful organizations, including successful schools, use the *Workforce of One* philosophy when it comes to developing talent. They consider each new and current employee on an individual basis. They work collaboratively to determine strengths, set goals for improvement, determine career interests, and share career paths that match those interests. "The most attractive and best organizations are those that have a reputation for developing people" (Cantrell and Smith, 2010, p. 22).

They provide professional development that is targeted to specific skills and they provide regular feedback for growth. Most districts have not traditionally developed people in this manner. In fact, traditionally schools have followed the sink-or-swim mentality and have lost many promising teachers in the process. Times have changed, and we cannot afford to lose any teacher with promise. The research today is clear. The quality and competence of the teacher makes the biggest difference in student achievement. However, we do not invest enough time, effort, and energy into developing talent in each teacher we hire.

GROWING TALENT

What actions can a principal take to develop and retain teaching talent? First, a decision that it is worth the effort is necessary. Then shifting the way professional development is delivered is essential. School leaders should forget the sink-or-swim approach they were trained with and adopt the "platinum rule" for teacher talent development: the premise being, do better for others than we would expect them to do for us (Reeves and Allison, 2009). According to Reeves, author of *Transforming Professional Development into Student Results*, effective teaching comes from practice in the classroom, with quality feedback for improvement. Developing talent in our teaching force is not about the all-inclusive checklists that administrators use for compliance. Rather, teachers develop skills by focusing on a few strategies that they practice again and again, with feedback from instructional masters on their progress (Reeves, 2010).

Reeves states that the components of deliberate practice include performance that is focused on a particular element of the task, expert coaching, feedback, careful and accurate self-assessment, and the opportunity to apply feedback immediately for improved performance (Reeves, 2010, p. 66). Robert Marzano is also a proponent of deliberate practice. He argues that teachers and principals in a school need a common language by which to discuss and describe instruction in their school (Marzano, 2010). It is this common language that allows a staff to know clearly what good teaching looks like and to establish learning goals for themselves to become effective teachers. Marzano states, "Expertise does not happen by chance. It requires deliberate practice" (Marzano, 2010, p. 82).

Michael Fullan also discusses the importance of deliberate practice. The characteristics of deliberate practice include:

- It can be repeated a lot.
- Feedback on performance and results is continuously available.

> - It is highly demanding mentally.
> - It isn't much fun when you are learning it (Colvin, 2008).
>
> (Fullan, 2011, p. 22)

Clearly, principals cannot provide this type of support alone. But, they can create structures and schedules that allow the most effective teachers and administrators to work with a small number of teachers in a community of learning around effective teaching practices. The principal should participate in these communities and have a small community with teachers of her own whenever possible. The leadership must create a climate where growth is valued and fostered. This requires what Carol Dweck calls a growth mind-set. Dweck is a renowned professor of psychology at Stanford University and well-respected researcher on the mind-set theory. In a growth mind-set culture, people believe that intelligence is modifiable, that people learn from mistakes, and that the brain gets stronger as we struggle through a challenge. In a fixed mind-set culture, people believe that intelligence is fixed. They believe that people have certain skills and abilities through genetics, and that some people have it and some people do not. If we are to genuinely develop and refine teaching talent in our schools, we must examine our current mind-set as leaders. If we do not have a growth mind-set and communicate it to our teams, we have little chance of seeing talent develop in our people.

It is recommended that leaders include talent development through meaningful feedback and deliberate practice in the school improvement plan, accountability plan, or strategic plan. Indicators of success should be created and tracked on a regular basis. For example, metrics could be collected on the number of mentoring hours, number of peer observations provided, number of support sessions provided to teachers, scores on climate surveys, proficiency levels of teachers as they work to master a few new skills, and the quality of feedback provided for improvement. When the quality and competence of the teachers improves, so, too, does the student achievement. Investing in the development of teacher talent will also increase retention and attract promising teachers to the school. Therefore, schools with well-recognized performance cultures will continue to grow and improve their results, and those that do not have cultures of high performance will continue to struggle. Finally, school leaders must realize that teaching talent is walking out the door en masse. Potential talent is not staying long enough to mature, and veteran talent is retiring. We must develop, nurture, and refine teaching talent if we are to provide a great teacher for every child in America (Curtis and Wurtzel, 2010).

SUMMARY
KEY POINTS

- The impact of effective teachers outweighs demographic factors in its influence on student learning.
- Talented teachers can be found in every school.
- Talent is the result of hard work, deliberate practice, feedback, and support.
- Too many superintendents and central office leaders fail to implement plans to develop talent in the teachers they have, and they fail to retain teachers who show promise.
- The United States is losing veteran and new teachers at alarming rates.
- A teacher shortage will soon impact every district in the country.
- Effective human capital management is the key to readying a district to compete for the best teachers.
- Principals are the key to creating and communicating a growth mind-set to establish a culture where everyone learns and grows.
- Time for deliberate practice and quality feedback significantly contributes to the development of teaching talent.

CHAPTER FIVE

HPC SIMPLE TRUTH 2: Leaders Cannot Do It Alone

No leader single-handedly ever gets anything extraordinary done.

Michael Fullan,
Change Leader: Learning to Do What Matters Most

In leadership circles around the country, this simple truth is commonly discussed; leaders at all levels will readily agree that leaders cannot make improvements alone. However, in school after school, district after district, leaders at all levels are trying to do it all alone. Very few leaders have well-developed plans to distribute and develop leadership among the people who work with them. Administrators and teacher leaders alike are reluctant to allow others to work on tasks that are within their *zone of responsibility*. Seemingly, they fear the loss of control or believe the quality of the work will diminish if they are not personally involved. In such a scenario, there is a limit to what can be achieved; even if every individual leader performs her responsibility well, she will hit a wall and achievement will go flat. In contrast, in a high-performance culture, there are leaders at every level of the organization and there is a deliberate and strategic effort to push all leaders into expanded areas of responsibility and higher levels of performance. In this scenario, all teachers are expected to be leaders and all leaders are expected to be teachers. The only way to expand and grow the organization's capacity for continuous improvement is to expand the capacity and knowledge of the individuals who work in the organization.

LEADERS AS MULTIPLIERS

In fact, the best leaders understand this well and strive to make everyone around them smarter. They are what Liz Wiseman calls *multipliers*. After a two-year study of more than 150 leaders, Wiseman concludes that leaders with a multiplier mind-set have significantly better results because they get twice as much from their people. These leaders have a rich view of the intelligence of the people around them, and they know how to extract and use the intelligence of the people in their organization. Wiseman found that employees who identified their leader as a multiplier gave 120 percent to their jobs every day. How did the multipliers build this kind of culture? Wiseman identifies four practices of the multiplier that have great relevance to building a high-performance culture in a school. Leaders who are multipliers look for talent everywhere. They watch and identify the native genius that people bring to the job. They label that genius and talk with the individual about it. They find a way to maximize the genius to the organization's benefit. Multipliers connect people with opportunities and shine a spotlight on their work. Finally, they remove barriers and let people do their work. Wiseman calls these leaders multipliers because they get two times as much from their teams. It's twice the productivity because the intelligence and capacity of people is amplified, which motivates them to work harder, seek challenges, and freely give their best. She states, "It isn't how intelligent your team members are; it is how much of that intelligence you can draw out and put to use" (Wiseman, 2010, p. 10).

Multipliers realize they cannot achieve ambitious goals alone; thus, they constantly seek to develop other leaders. In schools, this involves not only identifying and promoting aspiring administrators, but more importantly developing teacher leadership (Reeves, 2010). School leaders today must recognize how important it is to distribute leadership among staff members, because the simple truth is that there is too much work to do and one person cannot do it all. However, the problem has been that leadership is distributed *before* it is developed in the people who show potential and/or interest in new challenges. The results of the "tag, you're it" method of distributing leadership are frustration, self-doubt, and feelings of inadequacy among the very people we wish to support and keep in our schools. Richard Elmore warns against this haphazard method of distributive leadership. In *Building a New Structure for School Leadership*, Elmore contends that in distributed leadership, we want to avoid asking people to perform tasks they do not know how to do or have had no occasion to learn in the course of their careers (Elmore, 2000).

DEVELOPING LEADERS

Beyond the aspiring administrators in a school, which staff members should be considered for new challenges? Isn't teaching a tough enough job without adding more responsibilities to overburdened teachers? Harvard researcher Susan Moore Johnson argues in favor of additional responsibilities for *second-stage* teachers, those who are in their fourth to tenth year of teaching (Curtis and Wurtzel, 2010). Second-stage teachers have mastered the tough job of teaching. They are the ones best positioned to assist other teachers in the classroom by mentoring, modeling, and supporting newer and struggling teachers. They love teaching, but are looking for new challenges. They want to make a greater contribution to the school and their communities. They *need* a change to stay engaged with the work. Johnson contends that second-stage teachers are motivated by two drivers: to improve and to advance. At the second stage, they are coming into their own and they want leadership responsibility to improve instructional practice (Curtis and Wurtzel, 2010). These motivated teachers are the grease in the machine of the high-performance school culture.

Reeves agrees and argues that sustained capacity building for high-impact learning depends upon the development of teacher leadership. Successful teaching focus, including deliberate practice, videotaping, and incremental improvement in the art and science of teaching, depends upon teacher leaders who provide feedback to help their colleagues and who receive feedback on the impact of their coaching

(Reeves, 2010, p. 71). Given the current climate in education today, second-stage teachers will prove to be worth their weight in gold to their principals and must be supported and developed based on their strengths and individual goals, as well as the goals of the school.

Developing Leadership at George Hall Elementary, Alabama

The power of being a multiplier and believer in leadership development can be seen through the work of Terri Tomlinson, principal of George Hall Elementary School in Mobile, Alabama. She credits the school's remarkable success to the many layers of leaders in her school. She spends much of her time developing leadership among her team and feels confident that the high-quality work and dedication continues on a daily basis, whether she is in the school or out at a meeting (Education Trust Webinar, Sept. 23, 2010). George Hall was recently awarded the national Blue Ribbon Award, and Secretary of Education Arne Duncan visited the school and declared it a national turnaround school (Phillips, 2010). The turnaround at this school is commendable and worth noting, since it went from being one of the lowest performing schools in the state to one of the highest performing, due to smart leadership focused on developing talent and distributing leadership. This principal, and many like her, have learned important leadership lessons along the way. Leadership in high-performance cultures does not reside only at the top of the organization. It must emerge from, and cascade down to, those closest to the students, and it is incumbent upon these principals to build support structures and scaffold tasks for staff to develop, then distribute leadership at all levels of the organization. People who learn and grow together can conquer challenges that seem impossible.

DISTRIBUTE LEADERSHIP EFFECTIVELY

All school leaders would do well to develop leaders among them, starting with the second-stage teachers in their school, recognizing that each teacher has different interests, strengths, and career aspirations. Applying the *Workforce of One* concept to these valuable staff members will benefit the school immeasurably, if done right. That means knowing each person and matching the person to the appropriate task to develop leadership skill. Daniel Pink, author of *Drive* and *A Whole New Mind*, calls it the "Goldilocks" approach. He states we frequently have a mismatch between what people *must* do and what people *can* do (Pink, 2009). In developing leadership in schools, we must match the strengths and aspirations of each teacher to the task that will stretch but not overwhelm and frustrate her. This can be accomplished through deliberate practice on sharply defined elements of performance, but within the teacher's current job. Leadership development should be part of every organization's culture (Colvin, 2008). If school leaders do not implement a plan for leadership development, their collective talent will be squandered and the best teachers will leave to find positions that provide feedback for improvement and opportunities for advancement.

What follows is a sample Leadership Development Organizer, designed to help school leaders get started with this effort. The time devoted to the front end of this endeavor will pay great dividends in the long term, as more and more staff members are able to step into leadership positions, perform well, and contribute to the high-performance culture in a school. The organizer is not intended to be all-inclusive, but rather a way to organize the work and initial thinking. It can and should be modified to meet the unique needs of particular schools and districts. To start, list all second-stage teachers, veteran staff, and new teachers with high potential down the left-hand side of the chart. Then complete the chart by filling in for each teacher the number of years of experience, strengths, career interests, current leadership duties, development stretch task, the support person to guide her through the task, the review dates, and the progress results. This requires that the principal and/or school leaders look at each teacher as an individual and match her to the appropriate tasks. It also requires that principals talk with teachers to share the plan and learn more about where they want to start. This approach addresses Susan Moore Johnson's notion that second-stage teachers want to improve and advance. Figure 5.1 illustrates how to organize a plan for leadership development.

FIGURE 5.1 **Leadership Development Organizer**

Teacher	Years Exp	Strengths	Career Interests	Current Leadership Duties	Stretch Task or Duty	Support Person	Review Dates	Results
Jones	5	Excellent teacher Great rapport Strong classroom routines High expectation for self and students	Assist Principal	New teacher mentor Data Team leader	Lead development of school discipline plan	AP	Sept 30	

In addition to the Leadership Development Organizer, a sample assignment menu is provided to assist in selecting tasks that can be delegated, with support, under three major headings: instructional, operational, and organizational. It is important for school leaders to compile such a menu to keep track of what tasks are being considered and to whom the task is best suited. Principals should create their own menu based on what makes sense for their schools. Figure 5.2 provides an example of the assignments that can be made to stretch people and develop leadership at all levels.

Organizing and planning for the development of leaders within a school serves numerous purposes. First is the development of a strong cadre of committed teachers who contribute to the school's vision through teaching and leading. This development process satisfies the teachers' need for a sense of challenge in a job and for developing new

FIGURE 5.2 **Leadership Task Assignment Menu**

Instructional	Operational	Organizational
Grade-level chair	Cafeteria operations	School calendar—sports, clubs, holidays
Department head	Buses a.m. and p.m.	Master schedule
Data Team leader	Fire drills	Class coverage schedule
New teacher mentor	Inclement weather plan	Professional development logistics
University cooperating teacher	School safety plan	After-school tutoring coordinator
Curriculum development	Morning routines	Testing coordinator
Demonstration lessons	School discipline plan	Coordination of daily substitutes
Content coach; reading, math, etc.	School climate coordinator	Parent and community programs
Teacher support group leader	Student incentive programs	Data manager

skills. The staff will come to believe that they are seen as valuable individuals and that their work is being recognized as adding value to the school. Using the leadership development process will assist hard-to-staff schools by keeping good teachers and developing them to their full potential. The process also will attract promising new teachers, as word spreads that the school invests in the development of their teachers and supports them in their career interests and aspirations. Principals who invest in creating a reliable and consistent pipeline of good teachers and leaders are well positioned to meet new challenges and create a high-performance culture in their schools.

SUMMARY
KEY POINTS

- Even though it is impossible, leaders at all levels continue to try to do all the work alone.
- Leaders who effectively develop and distribute leadership throughout the organization increase the organization's capacity for improvement and extraordinary results.
- In high-performing cultures, leaders are developed and supported at all levels of the organization.
- Leaders must seek to develop, then distribute leadership in order to prepare people effectively for greater responsibilities.
- The best leaders make everyone around them smarter.
- Multipliers are leaders who get twice the effort and productivity from their people because they recognize and maximize the talents of everyone on the team for the good of the organization.
- Second-stage teachers are teachers in their fourth to tenth year of teaching. They are the best candidates for leadership development.
- Leaders should follow the Workforce of One philosophy to develop their people fully. This means identifying their strengths, matching their strengths with stretch tasks, determining their career goals, and providing experiences to help them reach their goals.
- Efforts to develop and grow leaders at every level will result in great dividends, as teachers will be attracted to a school that invests in their goals and career ambitions.

CHAPTER SIX

HPC SIMPLE TRUTH 3: Data and Accountability Are Critical Friends

Data is feedback to the system. Without data being collected at every level of the system, decisions are based on supposition, impressions, or blind guesses.

Brian McNulty,
Activate: A Leader's Guide to People, Practices, and Processes

THE FEAR OF DATA

At the inception of state standards and tests to measure student proficiency more than a decade ago, data were collected as a means of ensuring accountability for results. Educators at every level across the country were up in arms and extremely apprehensive about using a standards-based approach in classrooms, schools, and districts. Many argued that the standards and accountability policies stifled teacher creativity and individualism. Others argued that the standards and tests were a political ploy to make public schools look incompetent in order to make a case for charter schools. Fear set in as well, as teachers, principals, and superintendents anticipated embarrassment if their schools did not do well and the loss of jobs as a result of poor student performance. In the eyes of the public schools, data and accountability were anything but critical friends. The fear has since died down and a general acceptance of common standards has set in. The assessments that measure student proficiency and determine school effectiveness under federal and state accountability policies have become part of the educational landscape. However, the general acceptance of them as the best way to assess student learning remains in question.

DATA USE IN HIGH- AND LOW-PERFORMING SCHOOLS

As far back as 1995, Linda Darling-Hammond and Milbrey McLaughlin argued that habits and cultures inside schools must foster critical inquiry into teaching practices and student outcomes. They must be conducive to the formation of communities of practice that enable teachers to meet together to solve problems, consider new ideas, and evaluate alternatives (Darling-Hammond and McLaughlin, 1995). Since that time, districts collect more data than ever thought possible and, in fact, many suffer from data overload. What distinguishes high-performing from low-performing schools is the manner in which they organize, analyze, and act upon their data. High-performing schools have Data Teams and/or professional learning communities that follow a consistent cycle of inquiry into how students are progressing on learning goals and how staffs are progressing with their teaching techniques. Teachers feel empowered by the data and develop clear action steps to meet their common goals.

Conversely, in low-performing schools, teams of teachers and administrators claim to "look at the data," but without a set process or cycle of inquiry and little to no direction or training on how to proceed. After several frustrating meetings, with no clear plan of action for improvement, teachers fail to see the value of data analysis and teamwork and come to understand that both are a waste of their time. Since teams are meeting and data is being looked at, leaders make the assumption that data-driven decisions are being made and their school is functioning as a learning community. Never mind that they have never attended a Data Team meeting; never mind that they do not require minutes from the meetings; and never mind that instructional practices continue as they have since the 1990s. Since teams are "looking at data," the assumption is that they must be collaborative, high-functioning teams.

Several factors separate the high- from the low-performing teams. Schools with effective Data Teams have established a culture that values cooperation, collaboration, and teamwork. They have established structures, norms, and expectations for the work. The leaders of the school—principal, assistant principals, department heads, coaches, and, very often, central office staff—frequently participate in the meetings. They provide resources, structures, and adjustments to the master schedule to maximize the work of the Data Teams. They make the effective operation of Data Teams a priority. Under these circumstances, teacher teams engage in the regular practice of teamwork and collaboration, and they regularly track student and adult performance indicators to drive their work. The Data Teams process enables teachers to work together and learn from one another. The very structure of the Data Team facilitates the development of teaching talent, while providing opportunities for distributive leadership. The communities of practice discussed by Darling-Hammond are present in Data Teams and maximize the knowledge and skill of a collective faculty for improved student learning and achievement. This is an invigorating process that empowers teachers to act in the best interest of all of their students. Without the Data Teams process, teachers drown in their data and have no benefit from the experience. They are not learning or improving their teaching, and their students do not benefit from the collective knowledge of their teachers; thus, their progress is in jeopardy.

THE DATA TEAMS PROCESS

The primary purpose of the Data Team is to improve student learning (Allison, et al., 2010, p. 3). This is accomplished by improving the quality of teaching and leveraging leadership to facilitate learning for staff and students. The structure of Data Teams allows for acceleration and intervention in a systematic manner, and the process makes learning visible (Allison, et al., 2010, p. 4). The Data Teams process involves a six-step cycle. This cycle is followed consistently by the team at each meeting. The six steps include: charting and displaying data from formative assessments to illustrate the achievement of individual students on specific skills or standards. The second step in the cycle is to analyze strengths and prioritize the needs. Teams look concurrently at student strengths and weaknesses and draw inferences from both. Then they use the student strengths to build a bridge to address the weak areas. Step three in the process involves the teachers in determining short-term SMART (Specific, Measurable, Achievable, Relevant, and Timely) goals by which to measure the success of their instructional strategies. These goals detail current student proficiency rates, desired proficiency over the short term, measurement tools, and intended assessment dates. Next is step four, when the team selects research-based instructional strategies that the entire team agrees to use in their instruction, including how often they will use the strategy and the duration, based on the SMART goal. In step five, the team determines their results indicators, which provide them a vehicle to monitor their use of the strategies and determine the impact of their work on student achievement. Finally, teams monitor and evaluate results and determine if their goals were met. They start the process anew each time they have new data from their common formative assessments. Effective use of the Data Teams process can be the great equalizer for students, as it exposes the learning needs of each student and compels consistent, strategic action on the part of their teachers and principals. Figure 6.1 illustrates the six-step Data Teams process.

FIGURE 6.1 The Six-Step Data Teams Process

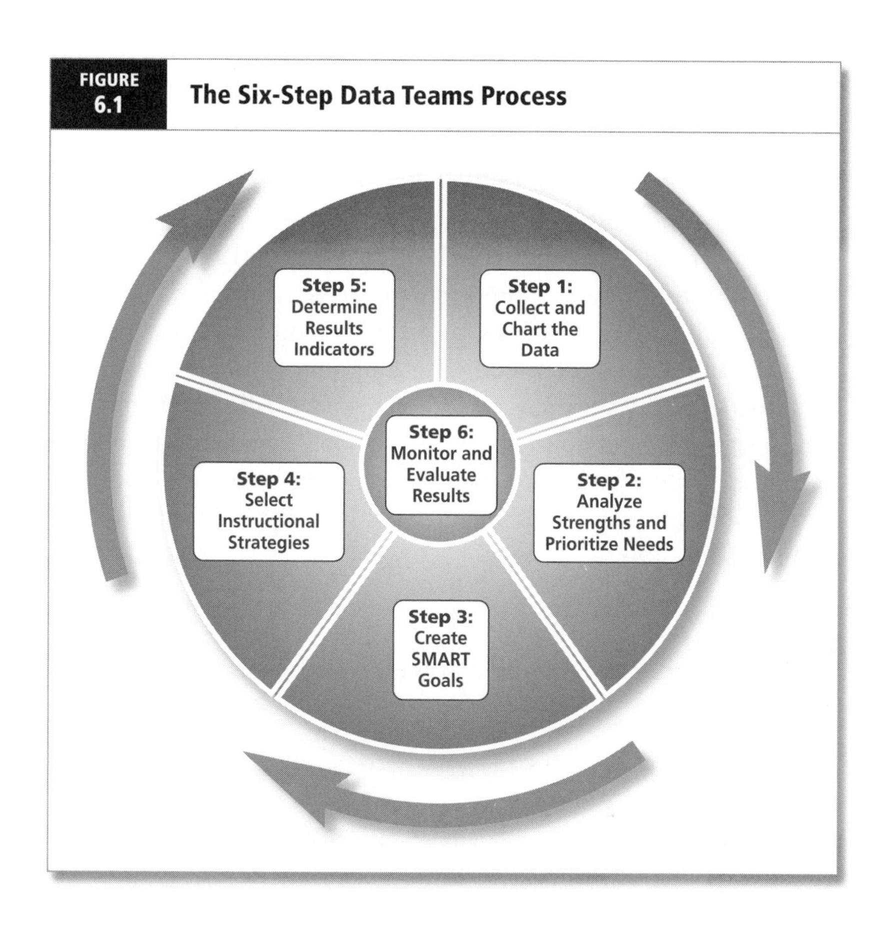

SUPPORTING DATA TEAMS

Leaders who successfully form highly collaborative teams know it takes more than just putting people together and expecting them to cooperate and collaborate. Rather, it requires support, practice, feedback, and a clear purpose. All teams go through various stages of development that school leaders must anticipate in order to have well-functioning teams. The most well-known model of team development is the one offered by Bruce Tuckman. In Tuckman's model, teams go through four stages of development. The stages include forming, storming, norming, and finally performing (Tuckman, 1965). It is important for team members to be aware of the stages they will experience so that when times get rough, they understand that it is simply part of the process all teams go through when first working together. Figure 6.2 illustrates the stages of team development from Bruce Tuckman.

In the forming stage, team members are generally polite, as they gain an understanding of the work the team is expected to do and where they fit in. At this stage, it is important for the principal or school leaders to provide clear instructions, provide structures such as a meeting calendar, and discuss the team's goals and objectives. Next, the team will experience the storming phase. In this phase, members confront their confusion about how to proceed, they question their leaders as to the purpose of the work, they experience the uncomfortable feeling of not knowing the process well, and they fear being exposed for not being competent.

FIGURE 6.2 **Tuckman's Stages of Team Development**

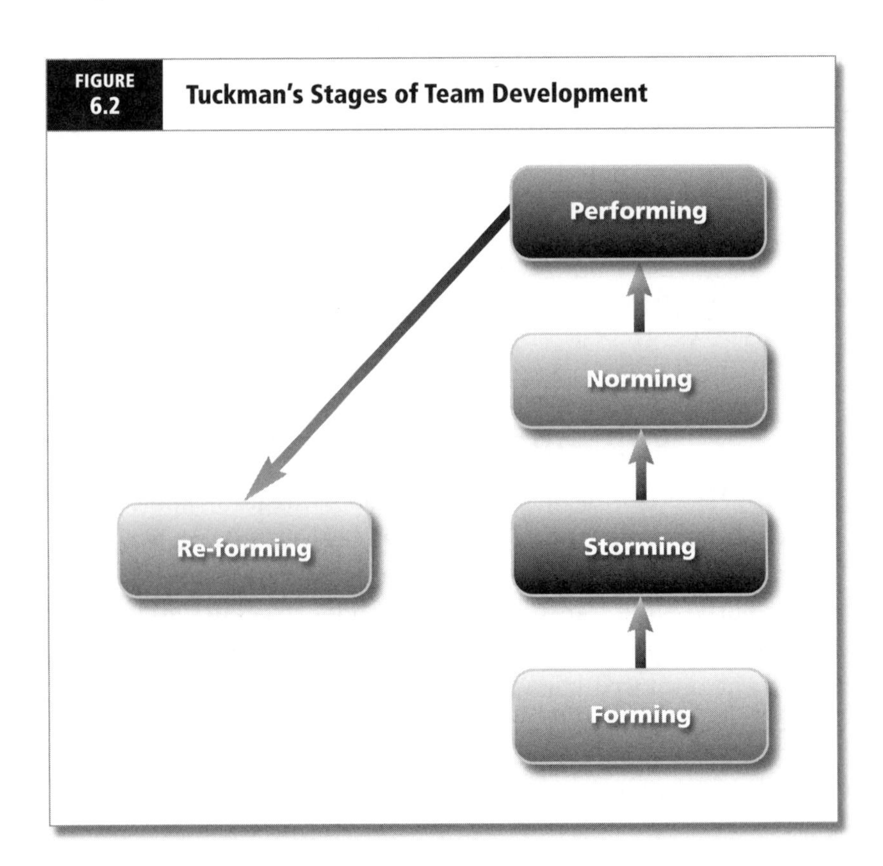

The leader of the Data Team must be able to persist through the storming phase of the work and reassure all members that they are learning something new and it will take a while to become proficient. Making mistakes is expected and learning as they go forth is the only way to become an efficient Data Team. As members become more comfortable with the process and learn from their mistakes, they begin to experience a flow or rhythm to their work, known as *norming*. They have a process. They follow the process. Their roles are known, and meaningful work is taking place. Finally, as all members gain their confidence and the work pace picks up, the team is in the performing stage. They have the process down, their data is driving their work, they trust one another to come prepared and follow through, and they feel energized by working together. A team cannot get to this performing stage, however, without the pain of experiencing the previous stages to get them there. If one person changes on the team, they go to the re-forming stage and start all over again.

Alfie Kohn, author of *The Schools Our Children Deserve* and *Punished by Rewards,* agrees that simply putting people in groups does not ensure cooperation and that turning a group into a team requires considerable effort and organizational commitments. There are such benefits to collaboration and teamwork, Kohn argues, that the opportunity to collaborate should be the default condition in classrooms and schools. People are able to do a better job in well-functioning groups than they can on their own. They are also more excited about their work. Both effects are due to the exchange of talent and resources that occurs as a result of cooperation (Kohn, 1999).

This argument is also supported by the research mentioned in Chapter Three and in the Aspen Institute's *Teaching Talent,* whose authors argue that principals are managers of human capital and leaders of learning. They must establish conditions for a community of adults to continually build the knowledge and skills that most effectively generate student learning. Building structures for teachers to collaborate, to improve practice, and to create a culture of continuous learning and improvement by effectively using data is critical to their success (Curtis and Wurtzel, 2010, p. 91).

Data Use at Ocean View Elementary, Virginia

One leader who has embraced the Data Teams process and benefited from great results is Lauren Campsen, principal of the 2008 Blue Ribbon Award school, Ocean View Elementary in Norfolk, Virginia. During the year it received this prestigious award, Ocean View served a population that consisted of 10 percent Hispanic students, 47 percent African American students, and 45 percent white students. The school also has a very high mobility rate due to the large population of military families and families with low-socioeconomic challenges.

Campsen came to understand the power of teacher collaboration and process-based inquiry around data. When the school won the Blue Ribbon Award, 100 percent of the Hispanic students and 99 percent of the African American students in grades 3 through 5 performed at a proficient or advanced level on the state Standards of Learning tests. The racial achievement gap has essentially been eliminated at Ocean View. For this reason as well as others, Campsen received the Terrell Bell Award for leadership.

Campsen and her team see data and accountability as "critical friends" to their school's success. She suggests that the principal is the key to successful teams. She states that a principal must know what challenges are occurring, who needs more support, what additional resources are needed and how the current ones are being allocated, and when to be ready to intervene before any potential roadblock becomes an obstacle to implementation (Allison, et al., 2010, p. 124). Campsen credits Ocean View's success to the consistent and proficient use of the Data Teams process at all grade levels. She shares that the initial implementation came as a mandate from her, but over time has become part of the culture and identity of the school. Every teacher in the school serves on a Data Team, which includes horizontal grade-level teams and vertical content teams.

Ocean View's high-performance culture was built from these teams over time. They have learned that the data is trying to tell them something about what they are doing, and if they listen to it, reflect on it, and give it voice, it will help them understand what to do next. The Data Teams process has built a collective efficacy at the school, and each teacher knows her work makes a difference in the performance of all students. Data and accountability for all students has been, and continues to be, the key to this school's success.

SCHOOL DATA AND ACCOUNTABILITY

Data and internal accountability fit hand in glove. "One essential lesson of the research . . . is that schools with strong internal accountability—a high level of agreement among members of the organization on the norms, values, and expectations that shape their work—function more effectively under external accountability pressure" (Elmore, 2004, p. 134). Contrary to today's popular view, teachers and administrators do not resist being held accountable for their work. But, as Elmore and his colleagues found in their studies, when external accountability measures are applied to schools, oftentimes they do not understand the full scope of what they are being held accountable for and to whom they are accountable (Elmore, 2004).

The isolation of classrooms and schools from state and federal education policy making, and the manner in which governments communicate with districts and schools, usually results in very little changing at the classroom level when external accountability policies are adopted. In many schools, accountability is determined by the individual teacher's sense of responsibility to the students and the community. Accountability is not collective or shared. But, in schools that respond well to external accountability, strong internal accountability systems are in place. These internal systems define the school's vision, mission, and shared beliefs. They link a few, but powerful, specific teaching and leadership actions to the vision, and they clearly articulate the accountability metrics, timelines, and responsibilities to monitor progress. The internal plan provides the staff clarity on the purpose of the work, what they are held accountable for, and to whom they are accountable.

ACCOUNTABILITY PLANNING

Douglas Reeves and colleagues at The Leadership and Learning Center have been assisting districts for years in developing internal systems of accountability, with great results. His book *Accountability in Action: A Blueprint for Learning Organizations* provides a framework for accountability planning. The framework engages an entire team at the district or school level in the development of a few, very specific strategies that are targeted and tailored to the organization's needs. Reeves argues that accountability for learning is much more effective than systems designed to punish and humiliate. He contends that accountability for learning equips teachers and leaders to transform educational accountability policies from destructive and demoralizing accounting drills into meaningful and constructive decision making in the classroom, school, and district (Reeves, 2005, p. 1).

A school-based accountability plan acts like a school charter that establishes the purpose and vision, the customs and culture, and the functions and roles of each member of the team. The accountability plan lays the foundation for the culture of the school and determines "how we do business around here." Not only will a few powerful strategies guide the actions of adults, the plan is constructed to build reciprocal accountability. According to Elmore, everyone is accountable to someone for their work, and each person holding others accountable has an equal and reciprocal obligation to provide support, resources, and guidance to assist those doing the work. Elmore suggests, "For each unit of performance I demand from you, I have an equal and reciprocal responsibility to provide you with a unit of capacity to produce that performance" (Elmore, 2004, pp. 244–245). The actions of adults are targeted toward improving student learning, and data is collected and analyzed on these actions to ensure a cycle of continuous improvement. In high-performance cultures, everyone knows the vision, understands their role in achieving the vision, and continuously builds their individual and collective capacity to perform tasks in line with the vision.

The most common mistake, and one made by most low-performing districts and schools, is including far too many strategies, goals, and initiatives in their annual plans. Many of these plans are hundreds of pages long and are so inclusive that it is impossible for any staff member to focus on a few things and do them well. The sheer number of goals, strategies, and initiatives proposed in most strategic plans actually detracts from the ability to focus, and it is often unclear how implementation will lead to improved outcomes for students (Harvard Education Letter No. 6, 2010). According to Elmore, low-performing schools do not know what to do to turn around their schools. If they did, they'd be doing it (Elmore, 2004). Thus, the 100-page plans with every educational approach known are created to give the appearance that they do know what to do and they are working hard. The opposite is actually true: a few strategies or vital behaviors, implemented well and monitored well, can go a long way in turning around an underperforming school.

Going back to the deliberate practice suggested by Reeves, Colvin, and Marzano, improving the quality of teaching improves student learning. Harvard Business School's Stacey Childress, quoted by Curtis and City, states, "Deliberate actions are puzzle pieces that fit together to create a clear picture of how the people, activities, and resources of an organization can work effectively to accomplish a collective purpose" (Harvard Education Letter No. 6, 2010, p. 170). Curtis and City also argue, "Without systems in place for discussing implementation, learning from it, and refining the strategy accordingly, the effects of the work are diminished and the plan becomes irrelevant" (Harvard Education Letter No. 6, 2010, p.172). And finally, Brent Stephens, quoted in the same Harvard Education Letter, agrees and states, "The manner in which a school describes the source of its poor performance is a telling indicator of its location on the trajectory towards internal accountability" (Harvard Education Letter No. 6, 2010, p.149).

An effective accountability plan enables a school leader to pull together all of the secrets and simple truths of a high-performance culture in a way that makes sense to everyone in the school. Internal accountability plans communicate the purpose-driven vision and mission, include strategies to develop talent in all teachers, describe how leadership is developed and distributed to individuals who are ready for a new challenge, and provide a structure for organizing and analyzing progress data for staff and students in teams where professional learning is of paramount importance. An accountability plan improves student achievement by improving teaching and leadership practices. The accountability plan creates the structures for a dynamic learning organization that continually assesses its own effectiveness in concrete and measurable ways. This is emerging as the core of local, state, and national accountability efforts (Curtis and Wurtzel, 2010).

Figure 6.3 is an illustration of how the school accountability plan serves as a charter for the core functions of the school. The mission, vision, and goals are all tightly aligned to curriculum, instruction, and assessment. Student outcomes are the driver for all decisions and data serves as the foundation for the work.

FIGURE 6.3 **A Comprehensive Accountability Framework**

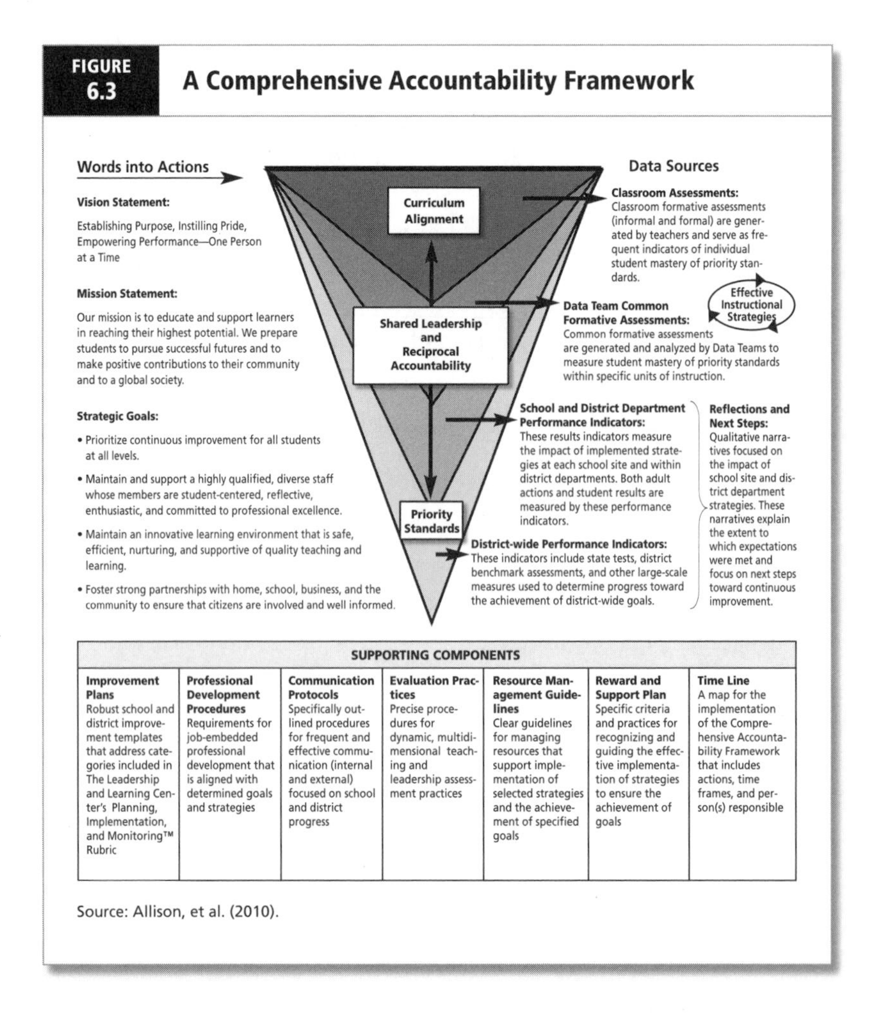

SUPPORTING COMPONENTS						
Improvement Plans Robust school and district improvement templates that address categories included in The Leadership and Learning Center's Planning, Implementation, and Monitoring™ Rubric	**Professional Development Procedures** Requirements for job-embedded professional development that is aligned with determined goals and strategies	**Communication Protocols** Specifically outlined procedures for frequent and effective communication (internal and external) focused on school and district progress	**Evaluation Practices** Precise procedures for dynamic, multidimensional teaching and leadership assessment practices	**Resource Management Guidelines** Clear guidelines for managing resources that support implementation of selected strategies and the achievement of specified goals	**Reward and Support Plan** Specific criteria and practices for recognizing and guiding the effective implementation of strategies to ensure the achievement of goals	**Time Line** A map for the implementation of the Comprehensive Accountability Framework that includes actions, time frames, and person(s) responsible

Source: Allison, et al. (2010).

SUMMARY
KEY POINTS

- Data and shared accountability are essential to a school's continuous improvement efforts.
- Teachers and administrators who analyze data together learn and grow together in a professional learning community.
- Teachers in high-performing schools are invigorated when they use data and collaborate with their peers using a set cycle of inquiry.
- The Data Teams process is an especially effective method to analyze data, create a collaborative culture, and address the learning needs of both students and staff.
- Schools and districts that have fully implemented the Data Teams process have benefited from outstanding results.
- The Data Teams process consists of six steps:
  - Collect and chart the data.
  - Analyze strengths and prioritize needs.
  - Develop SMART goals.
  - Select research-based instructional strategies.
  - Determine results indicators.
  - Monitor and evaluate results.
- Leaders must make deliberate efforts to prepare teachers for the stages of team development they will experience when they first start their meetings.
- Schools that create shared systems of internal accountability are well prepared to handle external accountability policies.
- A school-based accountability plan serves as a school charter and lays the foundation for a high-performing culture.

PART THREE

Applying the *Secrets* and *Simple Truths*

CHAPTER SEVEN

Facing the Challenges Ahead

The right drivers, capacity building group work, construction, and systematic solutions are effective because they work directly on changing the culture of the school system; the norms, skills, practices, and relationships.

Michael Fullan,
Change Leader: Learning to Do What Matters Most

According to the *Ivey Business Journal,* "Culture is the learned assumptions on which people base their daily behavior. Culture drives the organization, its actions and results" (Reid and Hubbell, 2005). The authors note that hospitals, financial institutions, government, and schools are increasingly paying attention to the effectiveness of their performance management, which includes creating a culture of high performance (Reid and Hubbell, 2005). However, many leaders, whether they are in business, nonprofits, health care, or education, demonstrate over and over that they would rather do anything than address culture as a core strategy for success. They consider culture a "soft" indicator, one that will come along once their strategies are in place and working well.

Nothing could be further from the truth. The literature in business and education, as well as analyses of published studies on motivation, human behavior, and leadership, are clear. High-performing organizations go the extra mile to create cultures where people are prepared for and expect change. The culture supports risk taking, expects mistakes during the learning phase, and supports individual and collective growth and development. Peter Drucker, the organizational and performance management guru, is credited with saying, "Culture eats strategy for breakfast." In this chapter, we will examine culture as a core strategy for schools and classrooms and why a focus on building a high-performing culture is essential to the success of all schools.

CULTURE CHANGE

Much has changed in public education since 2000. Public schools have become far better at collecting and charting data and they have disaggregated their data to highlight student achievement in various subgroup categories. Districts and schools have developed standards-based curricula aligned to their own state standards. Many schools and districts have developed or purchased formative assessments, aligned to their district and state standards, to regularly monitor student achievement. Teachers and administrators have begun to shed their isolationist ways and routinely work in teams to solve their student achievement challenges. Principals and teachers are increasingly placing the responsibility of student learning on themselves, as opposed to the students, their families, their socioeconomic conditions, or their home language. These changes represent significant progress in only 10 years.

Heifetz and Linsky categorize these changes into two types: adaptive and technical. Most of the change seen across schools over the past decade can be considered technical. Block scheduling, common planning, double-dosing in reading or math, new reading programs, new evaluation systems, school improvement planning, and collecting data are all technical changes. They require a change in the way educators *do* their jobs. On the contrary, adaptive changes require a fundamental change in the way educators *think and feel* about their work. Adaptive change includes what teachers believe is possible and how they view students who struggle, what limitations they place on themselves and the children, and their beliefs in their own abilities to make a difference. Adaptive changes have occurred less frequently than technical changes over the past decade. Adaptive changes involve changing the culture (Heifetz and Linsky, 2002). In the coming decade, most districts will have to go beyond the technical change level and delve deeply into the necessary adaptive level of change to affect the culture effectively.

COMMON CORE STATE STANDARDS

The demands of the next decade will require deeper, sustainable change, not surface change. At the time of this writing, 45 states and the District of Columbia have adopted the Common Core State Standards (CCSS). These standards were developed by educators from states around the country, with support from the National Governor's Association and Council of Chief State School Officers (www.corestandards.org). Having a set of national standards does not, on the surface, present a new challenge to the current and future adopters of the CCSS. However, the challenge will become clear once states and districts begin to "unwrap" the standards to determine the level of rigor and skill required to teach and learn them. The intent behind the new standards is to ensure that all students are college- and career-ready. The CCSS explicitly define what exactly it means to be "college- and career-ready." The characteristics of a college- and career-ready student are described as follows:

Demonstrates independence in:

- Comprehending and evaluating complex texts across a range of types and disciplines.
- Constructing effective arguments.
- Conveying intricate and multifaceted information.
- Discerning a speaker's key points; requests clarification and asks relevant questions.
- Demonstrating a command of standard English, including acquiring and using a wide-ranging vocabulary.

Students also:

- Become self-directed learners.
- Seek out and use resources to assist them, including teachers, peers, and others.

- Build strong content knowledge by engaging in works of quality and substance, and reading purposefully and listening attentively.
- Respond to the demands of audience, task, purpose, and discipline; appreciate nuances such as how an audience composition affects tone when speaking.
- Comprehend, as well as critique.
- Value evidence.
- Use technology and digital media strategically.
- Understand other perspectives and cultures.

(www.corestandards.org)

The Thomas B. Fordham Institute, an organization that has been studying state standards since 1997, released a study of the 50 state standards and the CCSS in July 2010. They found that the CCSS in English Language Arts are clearly superior to existing standards in 37 states, and too close to call in 11 other states. They found that only California, Indiana, and Washington, D.C., had existing standards that were clearly superior to the CCSS. In mathematics, they found the CCSS to be clearly superior to the state standards in 39 states, and again too close to call in 11 states (Carmichael, et al., 2010). As states begin to unveil their plans to implement the CCSS, districts and schools will endeavor to rise to new expectations and ensure that all of their graduates are ready for college and careers.

By 2014–2015, schools will be held accountable for results on the next-generation assessments, which will measure school and district success in teaching the Common Core State Standards to their students. The assessments are under development by two consortia funded by the federal Race to the Top program. The Partnership for Assessment of Readiness for College and Careers, or PARCC, and the Smarter Balanced Assessment Consortium, or SBAC, consist of national experts in the fields of assessment, instruction, and curriculum from K–12 and higher education. Although they are operating independently of one another, the types of assessments they are developing are similar. Each of the consortia plan to use computer-scored multiple-choice and constructed-response items, as well as some form of performance-based assessments. How these performance assessments are administered and scored may differ; however, both will challenge schools to prepare for assessments that are quite different from the multiple-choice item assessments most students have taken over the past 10 years. In fact, there is discussion about performance assessments that are computer–based, using a form of virtual environment similar to The Sims, or Farmville, or other programs that allow users to interact with the software in a real-life way. Imagine students logging on to the virtual environment to solve a real-world problem by using the mathematics standards they have learned, or conducting a science experiment with a virtual team of engineers. By 2014–2015, the assessments may bear no resemblance to those being used today.

Of course, the media, both local and national, will vigorously report the results from these assessments and provide readers with comparisons from state to state, district to district, and school to school. They will entice readers with headlines proclaiming states as best in the nation and worst in the nation. They will undoubtedly make the same pronouncements with districts and individual schools. In this environment, the pressure to perform at high levels will be of paramount importance to governors, senators, state superintendents, local superintendents, and mayors. This will result in intense pressure on school leaders and teachers to produce results.

RACE TO THE TOP

Additional pressure is brewing courtesy of the Race to the Top competitive grants being offered by the federal government. The Race to the Top program was released by the Department of Education in November 2009. The American Recovery and Reinvestment Act (ARRA) of 2009 provides $4.35 billion for the Race to the Top Fund, a competitive grant program designed to encourage and reward states that are creating the conditions for educational innovation and reform; achieving significant improvement in student outcomes, including making substantial gains in student achievement; closing achievement gaps; improving high school graduation rates; ensuring student preparation for success in college and careers; and implementing ambitious plans in four core education reform areas (U.S. Department of Education, 2009). The application criteria for states to receive a Race to the Top grant are:

- Adopting standards and assessments that prepare students to succeed in college and the workplace and to compete in the global economy;
- Building data systems that measure student growth and success and inform teachers and principals about how they can improve instruction;
- Recruiting, developing, rewarding, and retaining effective teachers and principals, especially where they are needed most; and
- Turning around our lowest-achieving schools.

Three rounds of funding have been completed. Thirty-five states and the District of Columbia originally submitted applications for the funds. Nineteen finalists made the first cut, and 11 winners were awarded money (United Press International [UPI], July 27, 2010). In the first round, Tennessee and Delaware were the lucky winners. Tennessee was awarded $500 million and Delaware was awarded $100 million. In round two, 10 additional winners were announced with all of the fanfare of a Powerball Lottery event. The second-round winners were: New York, Florida ($700 million each); Georgia, Ohio, North Carolina ($400 million each); Massachusetts, Maryland ($250 million each); and Hawaii, Rhode Island, and Washington, D.C. ($75 million each) (UPI, August 24, 2010). The losing states put forth great effort to compete for the funds, but they walked away with nothing. The state of New Jersey submitted a 1,000-page application. The state's governor, Chris Christy, grabbed headlines for his comments about New Jersey losing in the competition. As luck would have it, New Jersey along with six other states that originally lost in the competition have now been funded in the most recent round of Race to the Top grant awards. The other states include Illinois, Kentucky, Colorado, Louisiana, Pennsylvania, and Arizona. They received a much smaller piece of the original

$4 billion grant pot. The grant amounts ranged from $17 million for Colorado, Louisiana, and Kentucky to $43 million for Illinois. In total, $200 million was awarded. Most of the states plan to use the grant money for implementation costs related to the Common Core (McNeil, 2011).

This level of government spending during the nation's economic crisis has become a political powder keg. Every day citizens are unemployed at rates not seen since the Great Depression. Record-breaking levels of home foreclosures and congressional brinksmanship with the debt ceiling continue to challenge the fragile United States economy. Fueled by the media, who have their own survival at stake, communities and parents are demanding more for their investment in the public schools. A term not often heard in education before, ROI, or return on investment, is at the forefront of discussions on education both nationally and locally. Large urban divisions, where spending is high and results are low, are the focus of much of the attention. This point of view was poignantly illustrated in the film *Waiting for Superman*, where just a few schools were shown to have cultures of high performance or excellence (Weber, 2010). The movie offers viewers heartbreaking scenes with students and families trying to get into high-performing schools, only to be disappointed when not selected in the various lottery processes. The movie provides graphs and visuals that show a decline in America's ability to compete globally, and pushes a reform agenda. The film also takes direct aim at the two teacher unions and the teacher tenure system, as well as how teachers are evaluated for effectiveness. Following are the alarming statistics highlighted in the film (Weber, 2010):

- Eight years since the passage of NCLB, and four years left to reach the 100 percent proficiency goal, most states hover around 20 to 30 percent proficiency in math and reading.
- Among 30 developed countries, the United States is ranked 25th in math and 21st in science. When the comparison is restricted to the top 5 percent, the United States ranks last.

- Barely half of African American and Latino students graduate from high school.
- Most middle-class American high schools still track their students based on the old economy, but by 2020, 123 million American jobs will be in high-skill, high-pay occupations, from computer programming to bioengineering, but only 50 million Americans will be qualified to fill them.
- In 1970, the United States produced 30 percent of the world's college graduates. Today it produces only 15 percent.
- Since 1971, annual education spending has more than doubled, from $4,300 per student to more than $9,000 per student. Yet, in the same period, reading and math scores have remained flat, while they have risen in every other developed country.

MEETING THE CHALLENGE

Despite the grim statistics cited by the film, there are many outstanding schools in the United States. There are many wonderful, effective teachers who happen to work in low-performing schools. Researchers like Karin Chenoweth with the Education Trust organization have chronicled these schools in numerous reports and books, such as *It's Being Done* and *How It's Being Done.* These works show that schools are breaking the mold in the most unlikely places. The research being done at McREL, Harvard University, Public Agenda, The Leadership and Learning Center, and various projects sponsored by the Wallace Foundation also support the notion that high-performing schools exist in very challenging neighborhoods. How do these school leaders create performance cultures under such pressure? How do they keep pace with the ever-escalating changes and demands? What makes these schools high performers? What are the factors that enable them to work together, sustain commitment and engagement, prepare them for new demands, and propel them to higher performance, no matter what the challenge?

These school leaders know the secrets. They pay attention to the obvious simple truths and they take nothing for granted. They have created cultures that capitalize on the human emotion and internal drive for challenge and purpose. They focus all efforts on structures and practices that develop team members' talents by using a growth mind-set, and they use these talents to get results for the organization. These leaders have developed a leadership pipeline that sustains their work and outstanding outcomes, even when key people leave the school. These leaders have effective teams who are invigorated by working collaboratively. They are empowered to make decisions based on their data. Their people show a high level of personal and professional commitment to the purpose, vision, and mission of the school. They hold themselves and each other accountable for following the norms, meeting the expectations, and contributing to knowledge generation for all. They focus on a few vital behaviors that have been shown to make the biggest difference in student learning. These behaviors are identified both internally from the positive deviants and from the most current education research. These teams focus on the greater good and have a collective efficacy that makes a real difference in the lives of the children and families they serve.

SUMMARY
KEY POINTS

- Culture comprises the collective attitudes, beliefs, norms, and behaviors of an organization.
- A school culture can and should be changed when low expectations, excuse-making, and individualism are the norm.
- Leaders focus too intently on technical changes and not nearly enough on the adaptive changes necessary to change a culture.
- The adoption of the Common Core State Standards requires that school leaders examine their current culture and take steps to change it to meet the higher expectations in the CCSS.
- Pressure is mounting from the government, private sector, and parents for better results in our schools.
- Success in the future depends on leaders recognizing and using the secrets and simple truths of high-performing school cultures.

CHAPTER EIGHT

Building a High-Performing Culture Using the *Secrets* and *Simple Truths*

Cultural change gets real when your aim is execution. We don't think ourselves into a new way of acting, we act our way into a new way of thinking.

Larry Bossidy and Ram Charan,
Execution: The Discipline of Getting Things Done

As stated in the introduction, the purpose of this book is to inspire new thinking on the importance of school culture, and to empower school leaders to take action to build a performance culture in their schools. Of course, the next step for leaders is to turn inspiration into action by beginning to build a culture in their schools focused on organizational learning, teamwork, collaboration, growth, and determination for instructional excellence and high performance. Therefore, what strategies can a principal implement to apply the secrets and simple truths in their schools? This chapter is designed to answer that question. Readers will find suggested activities and strategies for each of the three secrets and simple truths below. These suggestions are not intended as an all-inclusive list, rather, they are intended as a starting point for school leaders. Many ideas for implementation of the concepts shared in this book will be spawned from starting with one or more of the strategies shared in this chapter. The research, from a wide array of fields, supporting a focus on school culture is overwhelming. Principals who act now, focused on the few but powerful aspects of culture from this book, will be rewarded with the joy and challenge of work with committed team members focused on a shared vision of teaching and learning, exceeding goals and expectations for the greater good.

STRATEGIES FOR *THE SECRETS*

Secret 1: Humans are driven to seek purpose and conquer challenges.

Conduct a Book Talk.

Start the conversation about motivation, purpose, and vision with a school team by conducting a book talk. School leaders can divide their faculty into small groups, with master teachers and/or administrators leading the discussion. Daniel Pink's *Drive: The Surprising Truth About What Motivates Us*, Jim Collins's *Good to Great*, Kouzes and Posner's *The Truth About Leadership*, or The Leadership and Learning Center's *Activate: A Leader's Guide to People, Practices, and Processes* would be excellent resources for examining this topic. Book talks are a vehicle for people to share their thoughts and ideas by discussing the content in the book. This approach also provides a common language for people to use that encourages discussion around new content and interesting ideas. It is also clear in the research that school teams that learn together publicly not only learn more, they also establish a strong culture around learning for the sake of improving.

Organize a Visioning Workshop.

Conduct a discussion with the faculty about what motivated them to become teachers. This is best done in small groups first to ensure that each staff member has time to share her thoughts on this question. Then have each group give a report on the common threads of their small-group sharing session. Each group records its themes on Post-it paper and hangs the paper in the room to be used in a group debrief with the entire faculty. From these results, engage the team in creating a purpose-driven mission in which every faculty member can find their own motives and vision. Ask questions such as, Why do we exist? Is this the best we can be? Why should parents send their children to our school? These guiding questions will focus the discussion on the higher concerns of education and engage teachers in a genuine discussion of their roles for the greater good.

Communicate the Purpose, Vision, and Mission with All Stakeholders.

Once the purpose, vision, and mission are clear to staff, the leaders must take every opportunity to communicate it through community newsletters, at PTSA meetings, and in weekly communications with staff. The vision should be articulated and highly visible throughout the building on banners and on posters in every classroom. All staff are responsible for making routine references to the vision. It is especially important for them to meet with the students regularly to share the purpose, vision, and mission of their school. Students need to be brought into the work and see themselves as part of the team working toward the shared vision and mission.

Provide Quarterly Reports and Recognition.

It is the responsibility of leaders to seek out examples of teachers, students, and staff who exemplify the purpose, vision, and mission of the school. At quarterly meetings, at a minimum, staff and students should be formally recognized for teamwork, cooperation, or focusing on the greater good. They may be recognized for reaching out to bring others into the work or for taking initiative to create unique ways to communicate and engage students and/or parents in the vision. They can and should be recognized for performance that aligns with the vision and mission.

Secret 2: A few vital behaviors can change the world.

Take Your Staff on a Treasure Hunt.

Organize data reports that show student achievement indicators by standards, subskills, subgroups, and by teachers. Determine if the school has some positive deviants that should be highlighted and analyzed. Brainstorm with the team on how to proceed with the greater staff. Solutions that can be generated internally have a much greater chance of hitting the intended targets. The positive deviance problem-solving steps are in Chapter Two, Figure 2.2. Follow these steps with the leadership team and then develop a plan for a whole-staff treasure hunt for positive deviants.

Create a Plan for Implementation of the Vital Behaviors.

Once the staff or a team of teachers have identified a few vital behaviors that they want to implement, it is important to clearly communicate what these behaviors entail and what supports will be in place to assist teachers as they learn. What professional development can be offered? What opportunities for peer observations and peer analysis of lessons will be provided? What resources can be provided? How will teachers receive feedback? How much time will they have for deliberate practice? This plan will be critically important to the learning of the teachers and, if done well, will help in establishing a culture of high performance.

Put Master Teachers to Work.

Assign a team of master teachers to analyze the 90/90/90 Schools™ research in *Accountability in Action* by Douglas Reeves, and have them develop a presentation for the staff on the common vital behaviors of the 90/90/90 Schools™. Ask the team to use additional sources to identify schools that are 90/90/90, such as *Bringing School Reform to Scale* by Heather Zavadski and *It's Being Done* and *How It's Being Done* by Karin Chenoweth. Have the teachers lead a discussion and/or self-assessment on the similarities and differences in practices between your school and the schools in the study. Also, have the staff identify one or two of the behaviors they would like to implement and have the presentation team create a plan to move forward with the staff's choices. The teacher presenters will need guidance and support from the administration.

Secret 3: Cooperation and collaboration are part of human evolution.

Engage in Professional Reading with the Leadership Team.

Share the *Harvard Business Review* article "The Unselfish Gene" by Yochai Benkler. Have each team share their views on the suppositions made in the article. Include in the discussion the norms of cooperation and collaboration at the school. Discuss the success of your professional learning communities or Data Teams. Brainstorm ways the leadership team can model effective cooperation and collaboration. Develop a list of ways to reinforce the efforts teachers make to cooperate and collaborate, including examples of teachers who put aside their individual needs in order to make decisions that benefit the entire school, grade level, or department.

Use the Common Core State Standards as an Instructional Tool.

Examine the Common Core State Standards in English Language Arts, specifically the speaking and listening standards, and pull out the standards that require students to collaborate, cooperate, make arguments, contribute to a discussion, etc. Create a rubric for each grade level using the standards that clearly outlines the expectations. Use your rubric at the next leadership team meeting, department meeting, grade-level meeting, or faculty meeting and score the team using the rubric for the CCSS. This can be a fun activity and serve two purposes: 1. Deepen the staff's knowledge about the expectations for students in the CCSS, and 2. Emphasize the importance of the adults modeling cooperative and collaborative behaviors.

STRATEGIES FOR *THE SIMPLE TRUTHS*

Simple Truth 1: Teaching talent makes the difference.

Organize a School-Wide Data Fair.

A Data Fair or Instructional Share Fair is an opportunity for the staff to highlight their most effective practices. The fair can be organized by grade level or department and will operate much like the traditional science fair. The guidelines for a data fair can be found in the appendix of the book. This kind of fair can be held on a quarterly basis and be scheduled to use data from quarterly assessments. The goal of the fair is to share and learn best practices from team members. Holding these regular fairs will increase the collective strength of the entire school.

Partner with Another School.

Contact a principal in your district to organize reciprocal visits for teams of teachers. Each school will ask the other to observe the implementation of a few vital behaviors or practices that they are working on and on which they want feedback for growth. The schedule for the day should include an opening session for the host school to provide the context for their work and rubrics or "look for" instruments for the visiting teachers to use as a guide. The visiting teachers will then go into classrooms and take notes on the implementation of the practices using the rubric. At the end of the visit, the teams come together to debrief the visit and provide feedback to the school on the implementation of their vital behaviors. Individual names and classes are not the focus of the visit. Rather, the focus is on team learning and team feedback. This activity exposes teachers to new practices and builds their capacity and instructional repertoire.

Simple Truth 2: Leaders cannot do it alone.

Conduct a Career Interest Survey.

In order to maximize the talent of the staff members and to spread leadership responsibilities across the school, develop and administer a career interest survey. This information can form the basis for how, when, and what leadership opportunities should be provided to various people on the staff. It is important to match people with stretch tasks that reflect their interests and talents. It is also important to select tasks that stretch but do not overwhelm individuals. One way to keep track of the development of leadership among the team is to use the organizer in Chapter Five, Figure 5.1.

Start a Leadership Book Club at the School.

Survey the staff for their interest in participating in a book club around current research and books on leadership in all types of organizations. Do not limit your book selections to educational leadership. At the first meeting, solicit suggestions from the club members and then decide together on the first book to read together. Team members should take turns facilitating discussions, which normally occur after reading one or two chapters. Teachers who desire to go into administration or become instructional leaders will appreciate this opportunity to learn and grow as professionals.

Simple Truth 3: Data and accountability are critical friends.

Create a Data-Rich Environment.

In addition to the data fair strategy, post school-wide benchmark data in the halls and in the main office. Post data in the cafeteria for students to see and discuss with their peers and teachers. Of course, do not put individual names on the displays, but rather post data by grade and standard. Design the displays to show a starting point and then subsequent points throughout the year that show growth. Have teachers post student data in their classrooms. Post more comprehensive displays in the teacher workrooms, where teachers can see the results for all grade levels and students. Many schools put the students' pictures on these displays to emphasize that the numbers represent real children.

Adopt the Data Teams Process.

Teachers accomplish more together than they do individually. The Data Teams process is founded on teamwork, collaboration, and professionalism. The six steps are followed consistently in each meeting. Training and support are required to fully realize the benefits of the Data Teams. The Data Teams process also empowers teachers to make decisions that address the needs of their students, as well as establish the structure for teachers to learn from one another.

Conduct a School Plan Review.

All schools are expected to have some kind of improvement plan. But many of these plans are focused on test scores only. To establish a system of internal accountability and a culture of high performance, a school plan should serve as a school charter—an agreement among everyone on the team of clearly articulated norms, vision, mission, expectations, and values. Goals and practices to reach the goals should align with the overall mission and the greater good of the work being done in the school. One way to review your current plan is to determine if it answers the question, Why do we exist? or Is this the best we can be? If the school plan does not answer these questions, a revision may be in order or an addendum considered.

Finally, conduct an assessment (see the Culture Assessment that follows) of the overall culture of the school as it relates to the secrets and simple truths of a high-performance culture. Use the results to determine first steps and develop an action plan for becoming a high-performance team.

CREATING A HIGH-PERFORMANCE CULTURE

Leading learning . . . means creating the conditions for a community of adults to continually build the knowledge and skills that most effectively generate student learning. It is an ongoing process of building structures and opportunities for teachers to collaborate, to improve practice, and to create a culture of continuous learning and improvement. The goal is not just to ensure that all individual teachers in the school are effective: it is to create a school environment where learning—for children and adults—is fostered, developed, and celebrated.

Rachel E. Curtis and Judy Wurtzel, Editors,
Teaching Talent: A Visionary Framework for Human Capital in Education

Culture Assessment

Statements for Reflection	Agree	Disagree
My classroom/school has a clear purpose-driven vision that is challenging and for the greater good.		
All work by adults and students aligns with achieving the vision and purpose.		
Our school has high expectations for staff and provides structures that foster team learning and collaboration aimed at improving instructional practice.		
My school values my work and provides learning opportunities aimed at my personal development in the profession.		
Teachers at my school have a sense of empowerment, teamwork, and community. They embrace new challenges with a can-do attitude.		
Teams at my school routinely examine student data, determine trends and patterns, and make agreements to implement instructional practices matched to the needs of the students.		
Teams in my school focus on a few vital behaviors and work collectively to help everyone implement them well and often.		
Our school routinely collects and shares data on the few practices to ensure deep implementation of specific strategies and to support all adults toward improving student learning.		
Our school has a plan for leadership development and I have had opportunities to develop my skills as a leader.		
The leadership in my school sets challenging goals and provides an equal level of support and feedback to assist teams in meeting the challenges.		
Totals		

Final Thoughts

Demands of greater accountability for student results and global competitiveness require that districts and schools address culture as a core strategy for accelerating and sustaining improvement. Schools and districts that continue to focus on the "low-hanging fruit" or technical changes will soon find themselves left behind and outperformed by colleagues who made the shift to culture as their core strategy for achieving higher levels of student performance. The secrets and simple truths discussed in this book can be found in high-performance schools across the country and the world. McKinsey and Company studied school systems around the world that had succeeded in going from good to great and that stayed great. They found three critical factors that led to consistent high performance in these schools. Their findings directly support the secrets and simple truths in this book. These three critical factors are: the establishment of collaborative practices; the development of support infrastructures; and the development of the next generation of leaders from within, ensuring sustainability, continuity, and focus on the purpose and vision of the school (Mourshed, Chijoki, and Barber, 2010). School leaders, both central office and school based, must recognize that a school's culture is what enables it to respond quickly and flexibly to challenges. It sets the tone, determines the work pattern, and dictates the level of effort individuals put forth in their work. The school's culture touches on the emotional longing in human beings to be part of something bigger than themselves and enables them to perform work for the greater good. Fullan suggests, "everything we know about motivation tells us that deep excitement comes from doing something worthwhile, doing it well, and getting results" (Fullan, 2011, p. 76).

Having a sense of purpose and engagement in a meaningful challenge alone does not make a school high performing. Time, energy, focus, and effort must be dedicated to developing the skills and talents of the staff. Teachers are leaving the profession in droves. We cannot close our teaching gap by simply recruiting more new teachers. We must develop talent in the teachers we have now and make career development programs part of the culture. This will serve as a magnet to attract more teachers with promise and will result in greater capacity to teach and lead. Leadership in a high-performance culture is shared. Teachers are leaders and leaders are teachers.

Progress in these areas, along with the progress of students in their learning, must be measured, analyzed, and acted upon by teams of educators. School-wide and grade-level Data Teams follow the same cycle of inquiry previously detailed. They use evidence to draw conclusions about strengths and areas for growth and follow through with instructional strategies designed to improve performance. Internal accountability plans provide the big picture and they demonstrate how all the pieces of the work fit together to move the school to greater levels of achievement. This understanding and collective efficacy is an adaptive change of great significance. According to Fullan, organizations that are successful are focused, have consistent leadership at the center, invest in frontline leadership and peer-based learning, and use data to confirm success and make connections (Fullan, 2011, p. 94). This requires careful attention and persistence. The institution of public schooling is a human-driven enterprise. It is time we learn what really motivates people to succeed and maximize our results by creating systems designed to reach people at their very core. Without the elements of a high-performance culture, new strategies have little chance of making a difference in the quality of our schools.

References

Adler, P., Heckscher, C., & Prusak, L. (2011). Building a collaborative enterprise. *Harvard Business Review,* (July/August), 94–101.

Allison, E., Besser, L., Campsen, L., Cordova, J., Doubek, B., Gregg, L., Kamm, C., Nielson, K., Peery, A., Pitchford, B., Rose, A., Ventura, S., & White, M. (2010). *Data teams: The big picture—Looking at data teams through a collaborative lens.* Englewood, CO: Lead + Learn Press.

Amabile, T. (1996). *Creativity in context: Update to the social psychology of creativity.* Boulder, CO: Westview Press.

Benkler, Y. (2011). The unselfish gene. *Harvard Business Review.* (July/August), 77–85.

Blanchard, K. (2007). *Leading at a higher level: Blanchard on leadership and creating high performing organizations.* Saddle River, NJ: Pearson/ Prentice Hall.

Bossidy, L., & Charan, R. (2002). *Execution: The discipline of getting things done.* New York: Crown Business.

Cantrell, S., & Smith, D. (2010). *Workforce of one: Revolutionizing talent management through customization.* Boston: Harvard Business Review Press.

Carmichael, S., Martino, G., Porter-Magee, K., & Wilson, W. (2010). *The state of the state standards—and the common core—in 2010.* Thomas B. Fordham Institute.

Coca-Cola Company, The. (2010). Mission, vision, and values. www.coca-colacompany.com

Collins, J., & Hansen, M. (2011). *Great by choice: Uncertainty, chaos, and luck—why some thrive despite them all.* New York: Harper Collins Publishers.

Colvin, G. (2008). *Talent is overrated: What really separates world-class performers from everybody else.* New York: The Penguin Group.

Council of Chief State School Officers (CCSSO) & National Governors Association Center for Best Practices (NGA Center). (2010). Common core state standards initiative. www.corestandards.org

Curtis, R., & Wurtzel, J. (Eds.). (2010). *Teaching talent: A visionary framework for human capital in education.* Cambridge, MA: Harvard Education Press.

Darling-Hammond, L., & McLaughlin, M. W. (1995). Policies that support professional development in an era of reform. *Phi Delta Kappan, 76*(8), 597–604.

Devane, T. (2009). The positive deviance approach—A briefing. www.positivedeviance.org

Doidge, N. (2007). *The brain that changes itself: Stories of personal triumph from the frontiers of brain science.* New York: Penguin.

Drucker, P. (1990). *Managing the nonprofit organization: Principles and practices.* New York: Harper Collins Publishers.

DuFour, R., & Eaker, R. (1998). *Professional learning communities at work: Best practices for enhancing student achievement.* Alexandria, VA: The Association for Supervision and Curriculum Development [ASCD].

Education Trust, The. (2010, Sept. 23). *Making sure all students learn: How one school built strong teacher teams and watched achievement skyrocket* [Webinar]. Featuring Agnes "Terri" Tomlinson, Principal, George Hall Elementary, Mobile, AL, and Kenneth Leithwood, Professor, University of Toronto. Washington, DC: www.edtrust.org

Elmore, R. F. (2000). *Building a new structure for school leadership.* Washington, DC: Albert Shanker Institute.

Elmore, R. F. (2002). *Bridging the gap between standards and achievement: The imperative for professional development in education.* Washington, DC: Albert Shanker Institute.

Elmore, R. F. (2004). *School reform from the inside out: Policy, practice, and performance.* Cambridge, MA: Harvard Education Press.

Fullan, M. (1993). *Change forces: Probing the depths of educational reform.* London: Farmer Press.

Fullan, M. (2011). *Change leader: Learning to do what matters most.* San Francisco: Jossey-Bass.

Gardner, H. E., Csikszentmihalyi, M., & Damon, W. (2002). *Good work: When excellence and ethics meet.* New York: Basic Books.

Goodwin, B. (2010). *Changing the odds for student success: What matters most.* Denver, CO: McREL.

Harvard Education Letter No. 6. (2010). *Strategic priorities for school improvement.* Cambridge, MA: Harvard Education Press.

Hattie, J. (2009). *Visible learning: A synthesis of over 800 meta-analyses relating to achievement.* New York: Routledge.

Heifetz, R., & Linsky, M. (2002). *Leadership on the line: Staying alive through the dangers of leading.* Boston, MA: Harvard Business Review Press.

Kohn, A. (1999). *Punished by rewards: The trouble with gold stars, incentive plans, A's, praise, and other bribes.* Boston: Houghton Mifflin.

Louis, K., Leithwood, K. L., Wahlstrom, K., & Anderson, S. E. (2010). *Investigating the links to improved student learning.* Learning from Leading Project: The University of Minnesota and the University of Toronto. Commissioned by The Wallace Foundation.

Marzano, R. J. (2010). What teachers gain from deliberate practice. *Educational Leadership, 68*(4). Alexandria, VA: ASCD.

McNeil, M. (2011). 7 runners-up finally share Race to the Top prize. *Education Week,* December 23, 2011.

Mourshed, M., Chijoki, C., & Barber, M. (2010). *How the world's most improved school systems keep getting better.* London: McKinsey & Company.

National Commission on Teaching and America's Future. (2010). *Who will teach? Experience matters.* Washington, DC.

Pascale, R., Sternin, J., & Sternin, M. (2010). *The power of positive deviance: How unlikely innovators solve the world's toughest problems.* Boston, MA: Harvard Business Review Press.

Patterson, K., Grenny, J., Maxfield, D., McMillan, R., & Switzler, A. (2007). *Influencer: The power to change anything.* New York: McGraw-Hill.

Pfeffer, J., & Sutton, R. (2000). *The knowing–doing gap: How smart companies turn knowledge into action.* Boston, MA: Harvard Business Review Press.

Phillips, R. (2010). Education secretary visits George Hall Elementary, says Mobile school is model of improvement. Mobile, AL, *Press-Register,* August 28, 2010.

Pink, D. (2009). *Drive: The surprising truth about what motivates us.* New York: Riverhead Books.

Po, V. (2011). Positive deviance: Combating high school dropouts. New American Media, March 7, 2011. http://newamericanmedia.org/2011/03/positive-deviance-a-program-to-combat-high-school-drop-out-rate.php#

Reeves, D. (2004). *Accountability for learning: How teachers and school leaders can take charge.* Alexandria, VA: ASCD.

Reeves, D. (2005). *Accountability in action: A blueprint for learning organizations.* 2nd ed. Englewood, CO: Advanced Learning Press.

Reeves, D. (2006). *The learning leader: How to focus school improvement for better results.* Alexandria, VA: ASCD.

Reeves, D. (2009). *Leading change in your school: How to conquer myths, build commitment, and get results.* Alexandria, VA: ASCD.

Reeves, D. (2010). *Transforming professional development into student results.* Alexandria, VA: ASCD.

Reeves, D., & Allison, E. (2009). *Renewal coaching: Sustainable change for individuals and organizations.* San Francisco: Jossey-Bass.

Reid, J., & Hubbell, V. (2005). Creating a performance culture. *Ivey Business Journal,* March/April 2005. Richard Ivey School of Business, University of Western Ontario.

Sparks, D. (2004). *Leading for results: Transforming teaching, learning, and relationships in schools.* Thousand Oaks, CA: Corwin Press.

Tuckman, B. W. (1965). Developmental sequence in small groups. *Psychological Bulletin, 63,* 384–399.

Ulrich, D., & Ulrich, W. (2010). *The why of work: How great leaders build abundant organizations that win.* New York: McGraw-Hill.

United Press International (UPI). (2010, July 27). *18 states, DC, race to the top finalists.* Washington, DC.

United Press International (UPI). (2010, August 24). *States win grants for education reform.* Washington, DC.

U.S. Department of Education. (2009). *Race to the top program executive summary.* Washington, DC.

Weber, K. (Ed.). (2010). *Waiting for Superman: How we can save America's failing schools.* New York: Perseus Book Group.

Whittier Union High School District. (2010). www.wuhsd.org

Wiseman, L. (2010). *Multipliers: How the best leaders make everyone smarter.* New York: Harper Collins Publishers.

APPENDIX

GUIDELINES FOR DATA WALLS, *or "The Science Fair for Grownups"*

Douglas B. Reeves, Ph.D.
The Leadership and Learning Center
http://www.leadandlearn.com/sites/default/files/resources/4fi.dt_.guidelinesdatawalls.pdf
(866) 399-6019

One of the most powerful techniques that educators and school leaders can use to improve decision making in the classroom, school, and district is the "Data Wall." Ideally, the Data Wall is a portable display, using the cardboard three-panel display frequently used for student science fairs. When administrators gather to discuss their ideas for improving student achievement, the Data Walls provide a rich source of information about the strategies employed in each school. Within each school, the Data Walls can be the focal point for faculty discussions on improving student achievement. For principals and teachers who are already using data to guide their instructional decision making, the use of a Data Wall will not create any additional work. For leaders who are not using data to guide their decisions, the Data Walls provide a valuable technique to jump-start their work. Most importantly, this technique will ensure that the analysis of student data is not isolated to a single seminar or a staff development program on data, but rather it becomes a continuous part of faculty and administrative decision making throughout the school year.

THREE ESSENTIAL PARTS OF THE DATA WALL:

1. External data, such as state test scores.
2. Internal data (classroom assessments or other school measurements involving teaching practices chosen by the school that reflect its unique needs).

3. Inferences and conclusions (drawn from the data).

INFORMATION FOR THE PANELS:

Left Panel: Includes tables, charts, and graphs that illustrate state test scores for the school and district. There may also be narrative comments, such as, "84% of our students are proficient or higher in mathematics according to the state test scores and 78% are proficient according to a district test. A review of the last three years of data shows consistent progress on both state and district measurements, with particular gains in the problems-solving portion of the math assessments."

Middle Panel: Includes data on teaching strategies associated with mathematics followed by another brief narrative, such as, "The charts above show that the number of mathematics assessments including student writing has increased significantly in the past three years. Those assessments have emphasized the problem-solving portions of the state test. The charts also show a strong increase in interdisciplinary mathematics instruction, with the frequency of math instruction in music, art, physical education, technology, science, and social studies much greater for the most recent school year than was the case in earlier years."

Right Panel: Includes inferences and conclusions, such as, "Our analysis of the data suggests that multidisciplinary instruction in math and writing in math have both been effective strategies to improve student performance. Therefore, we have planned to expand these strategies in the following ways (provide examples of the strategies specifically applicable to the individual school). We remain very concerned about the 16% of students who are not proficient on the math portion of the state tests and have developed individualized learning plans for each of these students. In addition, we have added the following intervention strategies for all non-proficient students (include specific strategies applicable to your school)."

OTHER NOTES TO PREPARE FOR "THE SCIENCE FAIR FOR GROWNUPS":

1. Principals will not make formal presentations—the Data Walls speak for themselves. Principals should be prepared to respond to questions from colleagues about their Data Walls.
2. The primary function of the Data Wall and Science Fair is to allow principals to ask one another questions and share with each other informally how they achieved their successes. *[If the Science Fair takes place during a multi-day leadership conference, then the displays should be set up during the breakfast of the first day and left up throughout the conference.]*
3. The process of continuous collaboration must continue all year, not just at the retreat. The Data Walls can be the focus of internal staff development, joint faculty meetings with other schools, and planning for instructional interventions and professional development activities.
4. CRITICALLY IMPORTANT: The Data Walls are not for the purpose of impressing outside observers, the superintendent, or any other external audience. The primary purpose of the Data Walls is for the principals to share information with their fellow principals and, most importantly, with their faculties.
5. Principals will have to make choices regarding which data to use. They will want to show the information that is most important, drawing clear conclusions, and making the point to the faculty members that they are not merely displaying data, but USING data to inform their leadership decision making.

Index